Out of the Ordinary

Out of the Ordinary

How Everyday Life Inspired a Nation and How It Can Again

MARC STEARS

The Belknap Press of
Harvard University Press
Cambridge, Massachusetts
London, England
2021

FIRST PRINTING

Library of Congress Cataloging-in-Publication Data

Names: Stears, Marc, author.
Title: Out of the ordinary : how everyday life inspired a nation and how it
   can again / Marc Stears.
Description: Cambridge, Massachusetts : The Belknap Press of Harvard University Press,
   2021. | Includes bibliographical references and index.
Identifiers: LCCN 2020021000 | ISBN 9780674743878 (cloth)
Subjects: LCSH: Festival of Britain (1951 : Great Britain) | Arts—Great Britain—
   20th century. | British literature—20th century—History and criticism. |
   Popular culture—Great Britain—History—20th century. | Nationalism—
   Great Britain—History—20th century. | Popular culture in literature. |
   Popular culture in art.
Classification: LCC DA566.4 .S685 2021 | DDC 306.0941/09045—dc23
LC record available at https://lccn.loc.gov/2020021000

For Freya

Only a man harrowing clods
In a slow silent walk
With an old horse that stumbles and nods
Half asleep as they stalk.

Only thin smoke without flame
From the heaps of couch-grass:
Yet this will go onward the same
Though Dynasties pass.

Yonder a maid and her wight
Come whispering by:
War's annals will cloud into night
Ere their story die.

Thomas Hardy,
"In the Time of 'the Breaking of Nations'"

Contents

Out of the Ordinary

INTRODUCTION

A Britain Forgotten

M Y DAD WAS AN ARTIST, so my childhood was full of pictures. A print of Edvard Munch's *Scream,* a haunting lady from Amedeo Modigliani, a terrifying Medusa: all of them hung on the walls around my bedroom in the little suburban semidetached house in South Wales in the 1970s. But I remember one picture more clearly than any other. It was a photograph of the dome of London's St. Paul's Cathedral towering over the firestorms of the Blitz. When I was about five or six, my dad used to show it to me at night and tell me tales of how the British people had stood alone in Europe against the horror of Fascism, remaining determined and committed to each other and eventually prevailing despite all the odds, tales that sprinkled a surprisingly proud patriotism into my usual childhood diet of bohemian counterculture.

At first glance, St. Paul's seems an odd choice as the setting for a bedtime story. I had never visited the cathedral. My parents never showed any intention of visiting it. But somehow with that picture, the great cathedral stood for people like us. Not for Britain in some grand, historic, untouchable sense, like Buckingham Palace, the Mall, or even the Palace of Westminster usually do. But for ordinary people. In those bedtime stories, I heard of the City workers who caught a glimpse of the great dome as they hurried over the bridges that crossed the Thames; of the commuters who saw it as their trains from the new suburbs pulled into the stations; of the people of the East End, many of them relatively recent migrants from horrors elsewhere, who lived with the beauty of the cathedral on their doorstep; of the volunteer firefighters, like my grandfather, who fought back the flames of the Blitz; and of those innocents caught up in the horror, like my dad himself, who had been born in a London hospital as the bombs dropped. Resilient there above the chaos, St. Paul's somehow represented all of them—no, all of us—at our best: standing together, unified in confident defiance, needing neither guidance nor charity, but capable of acting with strength for a good we hold in common that we cannot serve alone. Is it any wonder that I loved it?

These childhood sensations were no accident. Decades before my dad settled down to share them at my bedside, stories like these, often with St. Paul's at their symbolic core, had been consciously crafted by some of the greatest writers, artists, and cultural critics of the British twentieth century: the photographer Bill Brandt, art critic Barbara Jones, poet Laurie Lee, novelist and social critic George Orwell, novelist and playwright J. B. Priestley, and poet and radio essayist Dylan Thomas chief among them. For around twenty years, from the 1930s to the 1950s, they produced stories, poems, travelogues, magazine articles, photo-essays, wartime propaganda films, and radio plays that, read together or apart, offered a new and distinctive vision of what Britain was and what it could be. And they shared them with anyone who would read, watch, or listen.

At the heart of that vision were combinations of ideals that had rarely been thought of before. Through their prose, poetry, and pictures, they celebrated popular patriotism and tradition but rejected aristocracy, bombast, and flag-waving, what Orwell called "the Rule Britannia stuff."[1] They stressed the fundamental importance of national solidarity and a coming together across difference but were also deeply affected by local attachments to regions, towns, cities, villages, and communities, which Priestley dubbed "civic pride, vocal civic pride."[2] They rallied behind calls for bold social reform, stretching from the nationalization of major industries to the establishment of a welfare state, but they dismissed the usual mechanisms of politics through which others aimed to achieve those goals, whether the electoral wrangling of conventional political parties or the new revolutionary class conflict of the Marxist-inspired Left. They had no time, as Thomas inimitably put it, for those who "fall for the latest isms as gullibly as pups for rubber bones."[3]

Most of all, they rejected the standing of the "busy-body" bureaucracy of Whitehall experts and the "know-it all" opinions of the self-declared academic giants of the age. While cultural luminaries such as F. R. Leavis, Wyndham Lewis, and W. B. Yeats called for a restoration of traditional hierarchies and leading radical intellectuals including W. H. Auden, Stephen Spender, Sidney and Beatrice Webb, and Harold Laski turned to Soviet Communism, Brandt, Jones, Orwell, Priestley, and Thomas placed self-consciously humble, everyday humanity at the very core of their ideal. Theirs was an approach predicated on "an entire absence of cynicism or contempt towards one's fellow human beings."[4] Indeed, if any one argument summed their vision up, it was that ordinary people going about their ordinary lives possessed all the insight, virtue, and determination required to build the society of which they dream and need no direction by others. This is what Thomas called "our country," the essence of which was found not in the grand history of school textbooks but in "the pubs, clubs, billiard rooms, promenades, adolescence and the suburban nights, friendships, tempers, and the humiliations."[5] There is no greater power, Thomas always insisted, than the power of ordinary humanity itself.

This vision of the extraordinary, redemptive potential of everyday life caught the imagination of generations. In the Depression, novels like Orwell's *Coming Up for Air* and social commentary like Priestley's *English Journey* gave hope to those seeking to climb out of the economic crisis without giving way to either Communism or Fascism. In wartime, Priestley's radio *Postscripts*, Brandt's photo-essays of London, and Thomas's films provided stories of Britishness that always combined toughness and grit, on the one hand, with eccentricity, likeability, and a willingness to accept national failings, on the other. Later still, Thomas's radio essays, Jones's art, and Lee's poetry and prose offered an underpinning to the new peacetime social order, showing how promises for a bold, new future did not require revolutionary destruction but could, in Britain at least, be combined with an affirmation of the best of the past. And finally, the whole effort culminated in the great Festival of Britain of 1951, on which so many of these thinkers and their disciples worked. The festival was a mass, nationwide party "of industrial exhibitions, midways, art exhibits, concerts, carnivals and conventions," with more than 1,700 events in twenty-three towns and cities, which trumpeted Britain's victory in the war while affirming the role of the everyday people of the country in giving the nation its purpose and its meaning. "Other demonstrations here and abroad have shown a country's art, its industries and its institutions," the festival's official guide put it, "but none has tried like this to recreate a people's personality."[6]

Given all that was achieved, it is hard to believe that, just over sixty years later, this vision, the elements of which were so carefully crafted and the essence of which was so rapturously received, lies almost entirely discarded. Of course, the best travel writers and documentary journalists still pack Orwell's *Lion and the Unicorn* and Priestley's *English Journey* in their backpacks as they head out to explore the country for the *Guardian* or the *Daily Mirror*. Art students still study the compositions of Brandt and the criticism of Jones; indeed, the Tate Britain held a major exhibition inspired by Jones just a few years ago.[7] And theatre companies, television channels, and radio stations around the world certainly still put on productions of Thomas's *Under Milk Wood*, often populated with major Hollywood celebrities. But no one nowadays ties the pieces together. You would be very hard-pressed to find a major political figure saying, *this* is the society they were trying to build, we should try to build it too. And even if you cast across the whole country, you would find precious few dads or mums settling their children with tales of St. Paul's and the resilience of the ordinary people of Britain.

This disappearance comes in part from the fact that those discussed here produced no single manifesto or collective statement of purpose. They didn't write memos, leader articles in newspapers, or partisan policy briefs. In fact, they often refused to when they were asked. Instead they produced what T. S. Eliot called "prolegomena to politics": works that deal with the *fundamentals* that sit behind policy making, works that Eliot thought practical, day-to-day politicians "seldom read and which most of them would be unlikely to . . . know how to apply."[8] What this means is that it is hard to point to a specific shared concrete legislative proposal or a suggestion for reform and easy for lazy critics to decry their work as merely sentimental fuzzy thinking. In fact, they often appeared to be hostile to the whole process of politics.

The latter-day oversight is also due to the apparent failure of Orwell, Priestley, Thomas, and others to predict many of the fundamental challenges that confront our new century, from the pandemic to the revolution in gender politics to the possibilities and perils of multiculturalism and global migration, the decline of mass manufacturing, the rise of robots, artificial intelligence, and the potential displacement of millions of jobs. All of which, of course, is made worse by the fracturing of the union between England, Scotland, Wales, and Northern Ireland that the wartime generation took almost entirely for granted. This has prematurely aged much of the best of their work, allowing latter-day critics to dismiss it offhand as hopelessly out of date.[9]

Nonetheless, the fault of forgetting lies mostly not with the past but with us. It is the limitation of the ideological conventions of our own time that blinds us to the appeal of what went before. We have lost faith in the ability of ordinary people to shape the future of our country, even as the ravages of COVID-19 have reminded us more clearly than ever of the importance of everyday life. That's in part because the early twenty-first century has been a time of intense rigidity and polarization in political thinking—an almost unparalleled time of *us and them*—which stands in such sharp contrast with these efforts of the past. To eyes like ours that have acclimatized so thoroughly to divides between Labour and Tory, Brexiteers and Remainers, liberals and communitarians, cosmopolitans and nationalists, socialists and capitalists, working class and political elite, it is hard instinctively to appreciate a powerful tradition that not only was uncomfortable with such dualities but forcefully rejected them. Pick up a political column in a newspaper now, or watch a politically motivated film or play, and you will struggle to understand how tradition can be combined with progress, patriotism with diversity, individual rights with social duties, nationalism with internationalism, conservatism with radicalism. But it was in those combinations that enlightenment lay for those discussed here.

And it is probably not just a failure of perception or imagination that holds us back. It is a failure of political generosity and political courage too. For anyone who has dared to challenge these conventions of late has generally found themselves cast out by their group, denounced in social media as a "centrist dad" or in the equally strident terms of the contemporary lecture theatre as a political deviant. Within much of the dominant discourse of left-leaning academia, celebrations of nation are routinely denounced as essentially xenophobic; engagement with tradition is decried as sexist, homophobic, and otherwise socially exclusive; and even the ordinary routines of everyday life itself—routines that bring solace, comfort, and meaning to millions—are dismissed as irredeemably riddled with injustice and unfairness. This isn't an entirely new phenomenon—the American philosopher Richard Rorty powerfully pointed it out over two decades ago—but it has gathered almost unstoppable momentum in recent years.[10]

Freeing ourselves of this intellectual rigidity, and the arrogance that underpins it, is the vital precondition for appreciating the power of the vision that Orwell, Priestley, Thomas, and their contemporaries offered. But by itself that will not suffice, of course. Because separated as we are by decades of forgetting, we stand in need of a new, clear, and accessible account of that vision, one that is comprehensible to today's generations, which are being brought up, as we were, in a different, more skeptical age. That is what this book offers. In the pages that follow, my goal is to set out the fundamentals of this lost vision by teasing the ideas out from their original settings, where they can sometimes seem hidden to the modern reader, and revealing how the often apparently paradoxical commitments combined to render a powerfully coherent whole.

I start by examining the ideas these thinkers inherited from their predecessors and outline their reaction to them. I then take the core components of their own ideal one by one as they emerged through the 1930s and 1940s—with a chapter each on their ideas of community, nationhood, and politics itself—before showing how they were all assembled together at their great moment of triumph, the Festival of Britain in 1951, before it all fell apart with the so-called postwar settlement. Once the components are assembled in this way, we are able to stand back and see the pieces sitting together, revealing the pattern that makes up the whole and seeing what we can take from it for today.

From time to time, presenting the material in this necessarily formulaic way will do damage to the wondrous creativity, beauty, and drama of the prose and poetry to which I shall refer. It is hard to write clearly and succinctly in the manner of a manifesto without losing some of the magic. For that, I apologize. I hope, in part, that it is compensated by encouraging readers to return to the original texts and marvel at them anew. I note, too, that this book is not intended as a deep, scholarly exploration of any of the individual characters within it, let alone a biography of any sort. There are plenty of exceptional works of that kind already available. The task here is more polemical than that and in keeping with the kinds of works that Thomas, Priestley, and Orwell themselves might have written in a Britain torn apart by COVID and Brexit. I aim, that is, to present their vision of Britain to a new generation, one that could start the process of resolving the terrible tensions of our own times. For what follows is an account of nationhood that transcends those available today. It is an account that treasures the past but looks forward to the future, that cares for tradition but is hopeful about innovation, that is happy to look to its own people but also welcomes the world, that believes in the guiding wisdom not of elites but of all of us. It is one, in other words, that stresses most of all the extraordinary power of everyday life, one that notes that even in the hardest of times, every single day can be a festival day. It is an account of an ideal, in the magical words of Thomas, that shows our country as it should be "till St Paul's falls down, and the sea slides over the Strand."[11]

1

Getting Out of the Whale

*D*URING THE BRITISH GENERAL ELECTION OF 2015, I worked
as the personal speechwriter to the Labour Party leader, Ed Miliband.
Politics is a tough business, and there were all kinds of ups and downs
in that role. Most regular among the downs were disputes about what
was worth writing—or speaking—about and what wasn't. Many of
those disputes were utterly predictable. They had to do with different
views on the issues of the day: the economy, public spending, foreign
policy, immigration, and like. But one issue that I could not have pre-
dicted turned out to be the cause of particularly intense disagreements in Ed's team: the Second World War.

Although few people in the broader population noticed at the time,
Ed used to insist on adding a discussion of the war and especially of
its immediate aftermath to as many speeches as he could. The need
to tackle inequality and restore the welfare state? Ed would take it

back to the Beveridge Report and the cross-party commitments made at the war's close. Reform of the health service? He'd reference it back to the founding of the National Health Service in the 1940s. The true meaning of patriotism? It would emerge from a study of VE Day and the celebrations of Nazi collapse.

The reasons for this desire for constant reference were manifold. Ed believed the war was an issue that crossed traditional political boundaries, making a self-consciously radical politician more palatable to voters in the middle. He was also acutely aware that his own father fought in the war, having arrived in Britain as an immigrant, a refugee from the Nazis, and that made him immensely proud. He might also have had a faint memory of being told the kinds of stories I was told about what the country had achieved in the war. Nonetheless, as a rhetorical tactic it rarely worked. Audiences always used to stare blankly at him, utterly uncomprehending. I am sure I will go to my grave remembering an audience of seventeen- and eighteen-year-olds at a school in North London sitting with mouths open, clearly thinking: Why is this man in his forties going on about all of this stuff that happened nearly seventy years ago?

The real reason Ed's stories fell flat was not that they made him seem more elderly than he was but that, for most people in Britain today, he was talking about the wrong aspect of the war. For it is not the victory that British people remember with fondness. It is the privations of war and the peril of its very early years. It is the sense of Britain and the distant lands of its empire being left alone against the world, cast adrift by perfidious former allies and terrifying opponents. The myth of the opening year or two of the war that prevails is that of a heroic moment in dark times, bold leadership against the perfidious cowardice of an out-of-touch elite. Recently, in a speechwriting class I was giving, I played a recording of Winston Churchill's speech promising "blood, sweat, toil and tears" to a roomful of midcareer accountants at one of the world's leading professional service firms.

Some of them were so moved that their own literal tears joined Churchill's metaphorical ones.[1]

Proof of the power of that story is all around us in the general culture too. When the histories of our own time are written, the Hollywood awards season of 2018 will be remembered for one thing: the Time's Up and Me Too movements and the downfall of Harvey Weinstein. The memories will be of red carpets and black dresses. But in among the modernity was a lurking reminder of the continuing importance of the war. For the person who picked up all of the leading male actor awards was Gary Oldman, for his performance as Winston Churchill in *Darkest Hour,* and scrabbling along, picking up a technical award here and there and nominations for its director, was another wartime epic, *Dunkirk.* As Brexit negotiations unfurled in 2018 and 2019, the story of Britain standing alone in the conflict, proudly repelling German assault, emerged once again. It is these images, not those of D-day or the postwar reconstruction, that Boris Johnson turned to at the outbreak of the COVID-19 pandemic to try to inspire the country. And with good reason.

In many ways, the nostalgia is understandable. The sense of purpose, of determination, of pluck, excites us now in a time when we feel that we often lack these very virtues. But when the war actually broke out in 1939, it did not seem heroic to many, and certainly not to those who would later play their part in creating the very myth that we now remember so vividly. In fact, and directly to the contrary, it seemed that the war had no purpose and could lead to no desirable end.

"I can't raise up any feeling about this war at all," Dylan Thomas wrote to his friend Bert Trick in 1939. There was nothing in it worth fighting for, nothing worth sacrificing the benefits of a life of peace and relative stability. Not even anti-Fascism excited him. It is all a "fostering of hate against bewildered and buggered people," he thought.[2] For these reasons, and, it must also be admitted, as a result of a natural cowardice that he was never overly concerned to hide, Thomas spent the first few months of the conflict scrambling desperately to find someone to endorse his claim to be a conscientious objector, until eventually his own ill health came to his rescue and he was exempted from active service.

The more notable intellectual response to the outbreak of the war came in George Orwell's now much underappreciated masterpiece *Inside the Whale*, published just as the war was beginning. Ostensibly an elongated commentary on Henry Miller's *Tropic of Cancer*, *Inside the Whale* offers an intellectual history of the whole period sparked by the new hostilities. "While I have been writing this book another European war has broken out," Orwell wrote, and like Thomas he was clear that the prospects for such a war were bleak. Orwell possessed none of the Churchillian faith in the triumph of freedom and reason over an authoritarian foe. Not for him the patriotic excitement in blood, sweat, and tears or a sense that Fascism had finally met its match. All he could feel was a slow, throbbing fear. The war "will either last several years and tear Western civilization to pieces, or it will end inconclusively and prepare the way for yet another war which will do the job once and for all."[3]

The primary reason for Orwell's pessimism was his deep sense that even if Britain prevailed in the fight against Fascism, there was little prospect of a better future ahead. For Orwell, the late 1930s were a time of extraordinary pessimism. It was more than just a reluctance to put one's own life, or the lives of others, at risk that animated this concern. It was a sense that Britain had taken the wrong path since the end of the previous conflict. Although there was little doubt that Hitler was a grave evil, it was not clear what was being fought for. The years between the First World War and the Second, Orwell believed, had created two alternatives, neither of which had any appeal.

Inside the Whale lays out the charge sheet against the interwar years impeccably. In it, Orwell put the novelists, poets, playwrights, and associated thinkers who had shaped British culture in the years since the First World War on trial, as if he held them personally responsible for the horror that was about to come to pass. The 1920s and 1930s were a time of terrible ideological mistakes, he concluded, a period in which politics had taken wrong turn after wrong turn, leaving the country with almost nothing to stand for, nothing to care about protecting.

For our purposes here, it is vital to return to those mistakes. That is in part because we will see some striking similarities with our own times in these troubled decades. The division of politics into two warring tribes—one that placed the emphasis on a nostalgic longing for lost culture and tradition, and one that hurled itself into an eager pursuit of enormous economic and cultural transformation—will be familiar to anyone who has been watching Britain and much of the rest of the world tear itself apart in the last few years. But it is also worth returning to because understanding what had gone wrong is crucial preparation for appreciating the subtlety and richness of the alternative vision that Orwell and others sought to build as the war unfolded. That they were able to craft such an optimistic story of national renewal against this background should be the source of enormous hope for those of us who try to do the same now.

The task of this chapter, then, is to look back at the interwar years from the perspective of the start of the Second World War—to look, as Orwell had it, inside the whale as Jonah did when he was swallowed alive.

The First World War did not destroy the landscape of Britain as it did that of France, but the devastation that it wreaked was just as real. It led to a gigantic loss of faith in established institutions, political decision-making, social conventions, and religion itself.[4] "What was Christ in us was stuck with a bayonet in the sky," the young Dylan Thomas wrote to his first lover.[5] The period that immediately followed was one of great disorientation. The cultural giants of the time

captivated the world with their descriptions of the chaos that was unfolding, including James Joyce, Virginia Woolf, T. S. Eliot, Wyndham
Lewis, Aldous Huxley, and Lytton Strachey. The greatest of all the
chroniclers of despair in the 1920s, though, was D. H. Lawrence.

Long into the twentieth century, Lawrence's star still shone brightly
as a literary figure. But in the 1920s, his talent for politically engaged
cultural observation was unparalleled. Like nobody else, he posed the
intellectual questions that would determine the course of history.
Born in the small industrial town of Eastwood, Nottinghamshire, the
son of a miner, Lawrence scrambled throughout his short life to understand what was going on in a contemporary society that seemed
not only to disappoint but to dislocate the people who lived in it. The
much-feted promise of modernity, industrialism, and trade that had
captivated the Victorians and Edwardians was, for Lawrence, all just
one big lie, and his job was to call it out. For decades, industrial capitalism had wrought utter destruction on England and its people, Lawrence believed. It had built a "world of iron and coal, the cruelty of
iron and the smoke of coal, and the endless, endless greed that drove
it all." The First World War had revealed the truth of it in its barest
bones: "The cataclysm has happened, we are now among the ruins."[6]

Yet for Lawrence the horrors of reality were only the start of our
problems. The opening phrase of his later novel *Lady Chatterley's
Lover* captured the whole idea that animated his thinking perfectly:
"Ours is a tragic age, so we refuse to take it tragically," D. H. Lawrence wrote in that most compelling but misunderstood of novels.[7]
Lawrence's argument was simple. When confronted with the absolute horrors of war, with the Depression that followed it, and with
the blight of industrialism on the landscape and on people's lives that
had led to it, the British elite had not risen to the challenge, but they
had hidden, ignoring the pain, the suffering. And they had done so
in the most profoundly depressing of ways. They hadn't simply with-
drawn from life or pretended that things were a little bit better than
they were. They had drawn fantasies in the sky, painting imaginary

pictures of a country of the future, of a society that could magically be transformed as if without effort, whether by nostalgia, nationalism, socialism, Communism, or any other number of abstract beliefs. The empty, theoretical construction of a country "as it should be," and the fascination that people found in talking about it—endlessly talking about it—was the opiate of the time. It dulled the pain of a reality that was all around them but that was too much to bear.

Lawrence's most profound telling of this tale was his gut-wrenching short story "England, My England," published four years after the end of the First World War and worked on for many years before that. Here, Lawrence recounted the life and death of Evelyn Daughtry, an everyday middle-class Englishman, who finds himself fighting in an artillery regiment in France in the First World War. Desperately searching for some reassuring reason for his presence in the war, Daughtry finds himself playing in his mind with all kinds of abstract ideals: patriotism, soldierly authority, allegiance to the noble goals of freedom and self-determination. Over time, he learns how to play the role of the wartime idealist. He gives breath to the right kind of words, holds himself accordingly, and others respond to him. Even his wife loves him more as he mouths platitudes about conflict while wearing his uniform than she had done before.

In his quieter moments, though, Daughtry knows that there is no real truth to these so-called ideals. They are fantasies, based on empty rhetoric. And however hard he tries to reconcile himself to them, he cannot pull himself away from the realization that there is really nothing to them when compared with the actual, physical truth of his situation. Deep down, irrespective of the enthusiasms of others, he knows that brutality is the only reality of war.

Lawrence's story reaches its climax in an utterly breathtaking final few pages where Lawrence tells us of Daughtry's death at the front at the hands of a German shell. As the shell rips through his body and he lies in agony waiting for his own death, the two parts of Daughtry's being finally find open rage against each other. The abstract, idealizing part of his brain tries to bring a calmness, a sense of meaning and purpose to his own demise. "He sat there isolated, pure, abstract," Lawrence tells us, "in a state of supreme logical clarity," telling himself a story about why it was all OK really, and why his pain was justified by some noble cause. But before long, the settled, more genuinely humane part of himself realizes the actual horror of his own suffering and of the pain he will leave behind: "As he lay still, there came the knowledge of his wife and children, somewhere in a remote, heavy despair. This was the second, and deeper, reality."[8]

Fundamentally for Lawrence, this was not just the story of war and the empty lies told to perpetuate it. It was the story of the whole age. There was an absolute *obviousness* to what was really going on—injustice, environmental destruction, personal heartache—but no one had the courage to acknowledge it. They preferred instead to live in the fantasy of illusions of improvement. People of all kinds hid in their fantasies in their ideal abstractions, and they told themselves stories about why it would all be all right in the end. "This is all the trouble: that the invented *ideal* world of man is superimposed upon living men and women, and men and women are thus turned into abstracted, functioning, mechanical units. This is all the great ideal of Humanity amounts to: an aggregation of ideally functioning units: never a man or woman possible."[9]

If this was the diagnosis, his readers may have asked what he imagined to be the cure. If they had, they were disappointed. Although he was often tempted by political movements of different kinds, Lawrence gave up on a cure. The illness had progressed too far. "Socialism, conservatism, bolshevism, liberalism, republicanism, communism: all alike," he insisted.[10] They are captivated by things that do not really matter and worlds that cannot be. For Lawrence, the only response was to turn inwards, to personal life, to bodily satisfaction and immediate, often sexual, fulfilment. "What really torments civilized people is that they are full of feelings they know nothing about; they can't realize them, they can't fulfil them, they can't *live* them," he insisted, and you hear the urgency in the text even today. "And so they are tortured. It is like having energy you can't use—it destroys you. And feelings are a form of vital energy."[11]

Lawrence's desire got him into trouble, of course. But even if people did not follow him towards his personal brand of hedonism, he had without doubt framed the intellectual and ideological challenge of his age. "The time of change is upon us. The need for change has taken hold of us," he wrote. "We are changing, we have got to change, and we can no more help it than leaves can help going yellow and coming loose in autumn, or than bulbs can help shoving their little green spikes out of the ground in spring. We are changing, we are in the throes of change, and the change will be a great one. . . . And we are frightened. Because change hurts. And also, in the periods of serious transition, everything is uncertain, and living things are most vulnerable."[12]

Could anyone rise to this challenge? Could anyone enable it to tackle the horrific evils that beset it, without hiding in falsity, abstraction, and idle hopes and dreams? Could anyone help Britain find a new sense of purpose in the aftermath of the First World War?

Lawrence certainly wasn't alone in his ability to see through the illusions of his age. If anything held that unique generation of British poets, novelists, commentators, and ideologists that emerged after the First World War together, it was their belief that the certainties of earlier times needed to be upended forever. Not for them the Victorian confidence that the world was moving forwards, or the reformers' belief that the arc of history bends inevitably towards justice. Eliot, Joyce, Strachey, Woolf, Lewis, and their peers were "temperamentally hostile to the notion of 'progress,'" as Orwell would put it. "Here is life without God," they seemed to be shouting. "Just look at it!"[13]

Along with Joyce's *Ulysses,* it was, of course, Eliot's extraordinary poem *The Waste Land,* published in 1922, that was the most renowned statement of this decay. Eliot has provided generations with a vision of division and discordance, shaped in language that few have equalled since:

> In the decayed hole among the mountains
> In the faint moonlight, the grass is singing
> Over the tumbled graves, about the chapel
> There is the empty chapel, only the wind's home.
> It has no windows, and the door swings,
> Dry bones can harm no one.
> Only a cock stood on the rooftree
> Co co rico co co rico
> In a flash of lightning. Then a damp gust
> Bringing rain[14]

Eliot and Lawrence were connected by more than just a general sense of despair. There was something very specific that they felt was in decline. At the core of Lawrence's sense of loss, that is, was a craving for belonging. "The instinct of community was vital in his thinking," the great literary scholar Raymond Williams wrote in his inspired commentary on Lawrence. Williams described how Lawrence "attacked the industrial society of England" not in just a general sense but because it hindered the possibility of people coming together in a spirit of solidarity.[15] As Lawrence himself put it, the most fundamental of all modern capitalism's failings was that it "destroyed the natural flow of common sympathy between men and men, and men and women."[16] "We have frustrated that instinct of community which would make us unite in pride and dignity. . . . This is the side of the Englishman that has been thwarted and shockingly betrayed."[17]

Eliot agreed with that depressive diagnosis. But where Lawrence saw no obvious way out, Eliot possessed the faith necessary for a solution. For Eliot, what Britain needed was a spiritual reawakening grounded in a willing subservience to the power of tradition. What was needed was a public philosophy that was "at the same time older, more patient, more supple and more wise" than what had gone immediately before. Those who should lead, on this account, should be free of the illusions that had beset the wartime generation, and instead be "stout upholder[s] of tradition and continuity." Respect for tradition—the belief that the "vitality of the past enriches the life of the present"—was of particular importance here. The task facing society was to work out how "to concentrate, not to dissipate, to renew our association with traditional wisdom," as only by doing that could anyone hope "to re-establish a vital connexion between the individual and the race."[18]

Incongruent though it may be with our popular imaginary of the interwar years, this belief that a spirit of togetherness could be eked out of the contemporary morass if the British once again embraced traditions echoed across British cultural life. Eliot's journal *Criterion* was one place where likeminded advocates of the view could be found, offering the "achieved orderliness" that alone "make[s] life worth living."[19] But the view found allies even among those who otherwise shared little in common and who otherwise competed. The most revered exponent of the view at the time was not Eliot but the great literary critic and Cambridge professor F. R. Leavis. Leavis spent much of his enormous energy, as did his wife and their disciples, exposing—constantly exposing—the inability of the prevailing order to facilitate a sense of human connection, especially through his own journal, *Scrutiny*, which he launched in 1932, as a rival to *Criterion*.[20]

Leavis believed that what we now most frequently call community was almost impossible in contemporary society. Everyday citizens simply lacked the social sophistication, the awareness of mutuality, responsibilities, and obligations required to maintain it. In a brilliant passage it is worth quoting in full, Williams would later recall the experience of being in a discussion with Leavis and his followers when he was in Cambridge as an undergraduate:

> [Leading Leavisite] L. C. Knights said that the word "neighbour" in Shakespeare indicated something that *no* twentieth-century person can understand, because it signified a whole

series of obligations and recognitions over and above the fact of physical proximity. . . . F. R. Leavis was leaning against the wall and nodding vigorously (it was the time when this was *the* going position in Cambridge) and everybody was saying: *Yes, in the twentieth century nobody understands the meaning of "neighbour."* . . . I said I knew perfectly well what "neighbour" in that full sense, means. That got hissed—it was a remark so against the common sense that here was something in literature which was not now socially available.[21]

But what was the cause of the collapse of such communal awareness? Lawrence, of course, had turned his fire on the social injustice and environmental degradation of capitalism and the Industrial Revolution. Eliot would point to the decline of religion and to the separation between the words used to express ideas and the real spirit that animated them. Leavis and his colleagues at *Scrutiny,* though, found another force to blame. For them, the primary evil was what they dubbed "standardization." Behind all the evils we face, the same L. C. Knights wrote, "stand the cinema, newspapers, book societies, and Big Business—the whole machinery of 'Democracy' and standardization."[22]

Drawing heavily on the American social critics of the time, especially Stuart Chase and Irving Babbitt, Leavis and his colleagues were relentless in their charge that this was the age of the machine, the age of the mass, and it was in danger of losing all that was vital in the human spirit.[23] This danger was manifested in several forms. It was seen in the ugly and demeaning suburban housing encroaching on the revered English countryside, described variously as "drab and squalid," "scurf," and subject to "purulent beastliness."[24] It loudly exploded in the intellectually empty mass entertainment of the Hollywood movies and of newly popular music forms, like jazz and the blues. And it was seen most of all in the unwillingness of educators, journalists, and other noted opinion formers to challenge even the most mindless thoughts and beliefs of ordinary people. All of this was leading in the same direction, Leavis thought: to the removal of human zest, to a relentless deadening sameness. The more profound human qualities, the sophisticated sensibilities, required for deep, emotionally resonant connection with one another, with a place and a nation, were all being lost. In that context, it was no wonder that it was impossible to feel a sense of connectedness with a real, living, breathing human being.

What was needed for any of this to be turned around was an all-out assault on "levelling-down" and the reestablishment of distinction and of taste. Leavis wished for a world in which "it never occurred to anyone to question that there were, in all things, standards above the level of the ordinary man," a world where differences of quality were openly acknowledged and people found their place in the social order accordingly.[25] Of course, all of this drove a strong dislike of politics as normal. To Eliot, Leavis, and their followers, the leaders of all the major political parties were people who were unwilling to call out the deadening standardization of the modern age. This was true even of the so-called radical voices. Socialism and capitalism were, in fact, effectively indistinguishable in their political manifestations. What they offered were accounts of the world that were dull and boring, standardized and flat, empty of soul or a spirit. It was all too copybook, what speechwriters still call "boiler plate" today. We "can imagine a 'technocratic' or 'planned economy' too easily to find it an inspiring vision," Leavis explained.[26]

But even if this was an antipolitical creed, it was not an ideology of inaction. "To revive or replace a decayed tradition is a desperate undertaking: the attempt may seem futile," Leavis wrote in his opening *Scrutiny* editorial, "but perhaps some readers of *Scrutiny* will agree that no social or political movement unrelated to such an attempt could engage one's faith and energy."[27] And even if it did seem a hopeless task, a broad movement certainly followed. In responding to his call, a hugely diverse group of people, if ironically not Leavis himself, became obsessed with the utopia of a lost past, captured in such hopelessly romantic works as George Sturt's *The Wheelwright's Shop*, which described a settled social order before industrialization, where craftsmen paid homage to their fathers and their forefathers by continuing to practice time-honoured traditions of creation.[28]

The resulting movement has been described brilliantly in more recent years by the scholar Alexandra Harris in her wonderful *Romantic Moderns*. "Remembering the organic community was itself a communal effort," Harris tells us. "Writers, artists, farmers, social historians, musicians—all came to a shared recognition that it was the duty of their generation to bear witness to the dying arts of the countryside."[29] Photographers captured images of ruined castles and noble village churches; musicians wrote down the folk songs they imagined haunting country lanes; architects revived old decorative traditions, attempting to amend the harsher modernism of the times with a more parochial sensibility; eager anthropologists, mapmakers, and other, more amateur chroniclers headed off round the country collecting stories, celebrating old footways, and generally preserving whatever they could of times gone by.

The influence of this kind of thinking coursed far and wide. In many ways, it was the bedrock English culture for most of the interwar years.[30] It was no surprise that when the United Kingdom had to display itself to the world at the World's Fair in New York in 1939, it was to just this thinking that it turned. Among the various historical and constitutional paraphernalia, the guide to the British Pavilion celebrated the English countryside's capacity to generate "genuine communal feeling between men and women in different stations—the squire, the parson, and the schoolmaster, the farmers and the shopkeepers and the craftsmen, the farm workers and cottagers." The task facing all Britons, it concluded, was to ensure that "this feeling of a village community which is older than feudal times [and] has survived the fall of feudalism" can continue to flourish in the "democratic conditions of to-day."[31] Here, as the historian Jed Esty has it, was "a redemptive version of insularity, in which humane English values" were represented as "a sane alternative to the barbarism of Hitler."[32]

Although easy to mock, some of the consequences of this world-view were benign, even strongly positive. The poetry, painting, and architecture that this romantic modernism created often remain breathtakingly beautiful today and went on to leave a powerful legacy for the rest of the twentieth century, inspiring the giants of postwar English art Graham Sutherland and John Piper.[33] Leavis and his disciples also made admirable and extensive efforts to enhance educational opportunities for working people, rewriting curricula, organizing adult education classes, and encouraging a generation of teachers to seek greater levels of depth and achievement in their classrooms. The psychologist Marion Milner opened up new therapeutic avenues by turning towards the practical, lived experiences of normal life. And the protections offered to the countryside, such as the limitations on billboard advertising on the roadside, that Britain still enjoys today also owe much to this moment.[34]

For all its language of togetherness and spiritual uplift, however, what the unapologetic nostalgia also entailed, of course, was a deep distaste for the world as it actually was or at least as it was becoming, and that had far more worrisome overtones. In the mid-1930s, J. B. Priestley, who was not at all hostile to the romanticism at the movement's heart, recalled a deeply unsettling conversation he had with a follower of Leavis, a friend with whom he was staying as he travelled around the country. "He would have everything made by hand again," Priestley said of his friend, "restore the craftsman and banish the machine, replace the Trade Union by the Guild with its insistence upon a high standard of workmanship and if that meant doing without a lot of things, then we must do without them. . . . He disliked all our ways. He asked me to share his contempt for the new urban mob, the products of the industrial towns and free education at council schools and cheap books and so on and so forth; but as I consider myself one of these very people, I have to decline."[35]

There were undeniably political effects that were much more worrying too, however. Eliot, for all his intellect and wisdom, for example, spent much time corresponding with Viscount Lymington, the virulently anti-Semitic leader of the proto-Fascist group English Array, and gave succour to their efforts in his publications.[36] Knights similarly felt comfortable describing the bulk of his fellow citizens as formed in "large proportion of inferior material" in a manner that gave strong encouragement to those pressuring for eugenics.[37] And even if the movement did not always tip towards such evils, the general tendency of many English politicians of all parties to shy away from tackling the engrained social injustices of the age often found justification in the conservative nostalgia that flowed through this way of thinking. "Modern Britain still has her slums, her grimy industrial cities and sick and poor people whose needs are not yet fully met," the guide to the British Pavilion at the 1939 World's Fair read, but "no man can probe the future and no attempt has been made to portray the town of to-morrow."[38]

It is easy to understand, therefore, that from Orwell's vantage point looking back from the outbreak of the Second World War, all of this just seemed too much. Although there was something undeniably compelling in the vision that Eliot, Leavis, and others had inspired, the ideas that appeared naturally to have followed were just too negative and too exclusionary. There was no space in this thinking for gratitude, optimism, or renewal, no real space for hope or for belief in the power of people to improve the situation in which they found themselves. It all seemed a betrayal of the purpose with which it began, that sense of lost humanity, social connection, honesty, and the future. Orwell complained that if Eliot and his colleagues were "forced at pistol's point to choose between Fascism and some more democratic form of Socialism," they "would probably choose Fascism."[39]

If hierarchy and nostalgia did not offer Orwell, Thomas, and colleagues the purpose they craved, then we might have expected a resurgent group of left-leaning thinkers and writers to have done so instead. The 1930s was, after all, awash not just with conservative thinking but with socialist and Communist thinking too. Some of that was due to the phenomenal intellectual power of a generation of explicitly political writers, the likes of Sidney and Beatrice Webb, Harold Laski, G. D. H. Cole, and R. H. Tawney. They dominated academic discussions in the era of the Depression, and all of them tipped further and further towards the Left as the decade progressed. But the influence of the kinds of ideas they developed did not end there. The 1930s was an era of peculiarly public intellectualism. It was a time of discussion circles and reading groups, of the Left Book Club and of earnest young professionals coming together on weekday evenings in church halls and community centres to prophesy the end of the established order. The *Manchester Guardian* and the *New Statesman* made radical political thinking respectable in a way that it had rarely been in Britain before, as did David Lloyd George's transformation of the Liberal Party into the party of bold economic reform as the Depression deepened, under the guidance of John Maynard Keynes. By the time the war broke out, Britain had a full and stimulating socialist community scattered throughout the country.[40]

Most importantly, for Orwell and colleagues, the literary and artistic world had witnessed its socialistic turn too. In the 1930s a new group of writers arrived to challenge the ascendency of Eliot and Leavis, a group that Orwell described as "Auden and Spender and the rest of them," which was indeed led by W. H. Auden and Stephen Spender but which also featured a number of other compelling writers at different moments, including, but not confined to, those later known as the Auden Group, Christopher Isherwood, Cecil Day-Lewis, and Louis MacNeice.[41] With their rise, "the typical literary man ceases to be a cultured expatriate with a leaning towards the Church, and becomes an eager-minded schoolboy with a leaning towards Communism."[42] Together, they led what Leavis called, with regret, "the Marxising decade."[43]

For all of the emergent difference between this group and their predecessors, the starting point of this thinking was the same deep despair that had beset Lawrence. Everything had failed. The First World War had been a disaster, but so had all the attempts to respond to it. No government—Conservative, Liberal, Labour, or coalition National—had any answers. The country had endured a huge slump in the early 1920s and a polarizing general strike in 1926 and then suffered the fallout of the crash in 1929. Millions were unemployed. And the only apparent response the cultural establishment had was nostalgically to long for the return to tradition. As Spender himself put it, "One reason for the attraction of Communism was that the Communists also had a vision of final crisis, though they regarded it as one of capitalism rather than of civilization. Considered as an apocalyptic vision, the Communist view coincides with that of T. S. Eliot in *The Waste Land*."[44]

As the 1930s continued, this despair deepened, but with it grew the sense that a huge upheaval could result, one that could generate the vast transformation required, even if it came at the cost of violence and revolutionary insurrection. The Soviet Union offered some of that inspiration, but it was the Spanish Civil War that cemented this view. Here was a struggle that was open to an extraordinarily simplistic reading. It was, as Spender continued, "the only conflict to occur . . . in which clearly and indisputably the forces of good—the Republicans—were arrayed against the forces of evil—the Fascists."[45] What is more, it was actually open for young men to participate, not as members of a national army but as intellectual advocates of a transformative ideological agenda.

For many, the intoxicating excitement was overwhelming. Auden celebrated that "a revolution is really taking place. . . . In the last six months these people have been learning what it is to inherit their own country, and once a man has tasted freedom he will not lightly give it up."[46] Spender wrote, "I returned from Spain feeling more strongly than I have ever felt before that I support the Spanish social revolution. Since the war must be won if the revolution is to be retained there is nothing to do but accept it as a terrible necessity."[47]

It is Auden's poem about the conflict, "Spain"—"a serious application of the Marxist view of history to the Spanish civil war," in Spender's view—that best encapsulates the spirit of this group.[48] It is straightforward in its division between the present and the future, between evil and good. Now was the time of decay and destruction, conflict and contestation. Tomorrow would be the time of improvement, of justice, sociability, and human fulfilment. As a result, today was the time when the gloves should come off and conflict should be joined. Tomorrow would be the moment when harmony could prevail. Reading it now, it is easy to see the poem as parody:

> To-morrow the rediscovery of romantic love,
> the photographing of ravens; all the fun under
> Liberty's masterful shadow;
> To-morrow the hour of the pageant-master and the musician,
> The beautiful roar of the chorus under the dome;
> To-morrow the exchanging of tips on the breeding of terriers,
> The eager election of chairmen
> By the sudden forest of hands. But to-day the struggle.
> To-morrow for the young the poets exploding like bombs,
> The walks by the lake, the weeks of perfect communion;
> To-morrow the bicycle races
> Through the suburbs on summer evenings. But to-day the
>   struggle.
> To-day the deliberate increase in the chances of death,
> The conscious acceptance of guilt in the necessary murder.[49]

To Orwell, himself a veteran of the civil war when he read these words, this was empty, dishonest, blind to the dangers of violence and authoritarianism. Its simplistic sense of the ends justifying the means opened the door to horrific social consequences, with human beings being discounted as mere collateral damage in the struggle for social change. That chilling phrase "necessary murder" was the one for which Orwell could never forgive Auden. We can understand why even from the perspective of our own times, but it is all the more chilling still when put against the context of the gulags and concentration camps then spreading across Europe and the world.

Doubts about actually existing Communism did creep in on the intellectual British Left as the interwar years progressed, as they did also with some of the professional political thinkers like Laski and the Webbs. There was much hullabaloo in 1937, for example, when the International Writers' Congress in Madrid responded to André Gide's *Retour de l'URSS*—an exposé of what was going on in the Soviet Union. Spender later recalled writing to Gide—privately, of course—to say that he had his support and that the USSR had crossed a line in its infringements on human decency. Spender believed that Auden took this view too, though again precious little was said in public at the time.[50] Certainly, by the outbreak of the war, the scales were beginning to fall away, and Stalin's pact with Hitler would, of course, strip them still further.

None of this, though, did anything to reassure Orwell or those who shared his sensibilities. It wasn't the attitude to Communism, authoritarianism or even violence per se that was the problem to Orwell. It was the whole ethos that lay behind it. It was the smugness, the self-satisfaction, the sense of moral and intellectual superiority that mattered most, what Orwell called the "Boy Scout atmosphere of bare knees and community singing."[51] There was no real sense of community, of solidarity, of deep human feeling with people from beyond the movement. It just all seemed so fake.[52]

Without knowing Orwell's work, Thomas wrote about the intellectual socialist scene of the 1930s in very similar terms. Having left South Wales to try to mingle with the intellectual elite of the age in London after the publication of his first collection of poems, Thomas was desperately disappointed by what he found. This was a crowd of "pseudo-artists," he wrote to his friend Bert Trick, the owner of a small grocery store in Thomas's hometown who had himself been an eager follower of left-leaning intellectual trends from afar. It was full of "beards, of the naught expressions of an entirely outmoded period of artistic importance," led by people who threw "the most boring Bohemian parties that I have ever thought possible." These people, Thomas continued, were just "little maggots," secure in their own sense of moral superiority but knowing nothing of the real, daily struggles to which they pledged allegiance.[53] Unsurprisingly he felt their work betrayed these failings too. And the worst of all of them was the most celebrated, Auden. The "emotional appeal in Auden wouldn't raise a corresponding emotion in a tick," Thomas insisted.[54] Auden "writes like Disney." "He knows the shape of beasts" but "he does not know what shapes or motivates those beasts." And, also like Disney, he, in fact, "might have a company of artists producing his best lines."[55]

All this was exactly what Lawrence had drawn attention to back in the 1920s, of course. Just like the thinkers that he mocked in *Lady Chatterley's Lover* and elsewhere, these socialist intellectuals were obsessed with "the system" rather than with the people who made it up. They were clear about that too. "To be modern," Spender lectured, means "to interpret the poet's individual experience of lived history in light of some kind of Marxist analysis."[56] But this focus took them far away from the actual lives of actual people. They were left with what Orwell would later call "the emotional shallowness of people who live in a world of ideas and have little contact with physical reality."[57] Lawrence again had been astonishingly prescient when it came to precisely these tendencies. "They care! They simply are eaten up with caring," he had written. "They are so busy caring . . . that they never know where they are. They certainly never live on the spot where they are. They inhabit abstract space, the desert void of politics, principles, right and wrong, and so forth. They are doomed to be abstract. Talking to them is like trying to have a human relationship with the letter x in algebra."[58]

The paradox was clear. Although the socialists claimed to be committed to the interests of ordinary people—what they called the proletariat or the working class—they were in fact "always completely removed from the working class in idiom and manner of thought."[59] What was less clear was why they bothered at all. That was the question that continually confounded Orwell. "Sometimes I look at a Socialist—the intellectual, tract-writing type of Socialist, with his pullover, his fuzzy hair, and his Marxian quotation—and wonder what the devil his motive really *is*," Orwell said. Perhaps it was just to have "simply something to believe in," or perhaps it was "a hypertrophied sense of order. The present state of affairs . . . because it is untidy; what they desire, basically, is to reduce the world to something resembling a chessboard."[60]

These explanations might well have spoken to some, but the fundamental reality was simpler than they suggested. At least much of the time, the failings of 1930s socialism were a straightforward reflection of the class, experience, and self-interest of the socialist writers themselves, the vast majority of whom fell into a "public-school-university-Bloomsbury pattern" that distanced them dramatically from the bulk of society.[61] As Spender himself would later admit, their writing was often directly addressed only "to sixth formers from their old schools and to one another."[62] Occasionally, they agonized about just this, but even then they did so in ways that tended simply to emphasize the problem. "The artist today feels himself totally submerged by bourgeois tradition," Spender said, "he feels that nothing he can write could possibly appeal to a proletarian audience, and therefore he finds himself becoming simply the bourgeois artist in revolt."[63]

Even those who enjoyed this degree of self-awareness concluded that there was nothing to be done because of the contempt in which they held most working people themselves. "The artist cannot renounce the bourgeois tradition because the proletariat has no alternative tradition which he could adopt," Spender complained. If only ordinary people were not so stupid, base, free of sophistication and intellectual awareness, then artists of the Left could immerse themselves in their world. As it was, ordinary Britons appeared to believe in "Stanley Baldwin's premiership, the Royal Jubilee, the British Empire Exhibition," each of them an experience that it was implied could never appeal to those of finer sensibilities and more sophisticated political tastes.[64]

Britain had been left ideologically bereft by its dominant intellectual traditions in the years between the wars. Faced with the unprecedented challenge of a global conflict with Fascism, those seeking intellectual direction from established authorities were left with an unenviable choice. Either they could opt for a philosophy grounded in a longing for a world that had been lost (or that had never been), a world of natural hierarchy, unquestioned tradition, and communal harmony between people "who knew their station," or they could turn to an increasingly breathless, smug, and dangerously self-satisfied socialism—a philosophy that was willing to appease violent authoritarianism as long as it was from those on the "right side of history" and that expressly believed that "the system" mattered more than the individual human beings of which it was composed. Weighing it all up, as the Second World War took hold, Orwell was damning: "Progress and reaction have both turned out to be swindles."[65]

Was there an alternative? As the outbreak of war rocked him, Orwell wrote in increasingly pessimistic terms, as did others around him. It was as if Lawrence's much-predicted moment of complete and final cataclysm—the *apocalypse*—had arrived. But in fact, the closing pages of *Inside the Whale* offered the hint of something both more optimistic and more profound. The common problem in both the prevailing intellectual traditions, Orwell observed, was that they were fundamentally dissatisfied with the world as it is and were seeking all the time to upend it. Leavis called for the restoration of "standards above the level of the ordinary man," and Spender wished to overcome

the intellectual and ideological limitations of those very same
people. Neither was capable of sitting back and looking at the world
as it is from the perspective of those who do not imagine themselves
to be in a position to throw everything up in the air and start again,
but who just live. Wasn't it possible instead to be a Jonah, Orwell
asked, to write and think like a "willing Jonah," someone swallowed by the whale, not struggling to escape to some imagined alternative, but capable of looking around himself and making sense of
the circumstances in which he lay? "Get inside the whale (for you *are*,
of course). Give yourself over to the world-process, stop fighting
against it or pretending that you control it; simply accept it, endure
it, record it."[66]

Although Orwell presented this thought as an epiphany in *Inside
the Whale*, it was not unique. Wasn't this, after all, what Lawrence
had really been calling for all along? The ability to look at the world
as it is, mentally and emotionally to withstand its horrors, and to find
joy in the real beauty that remained there, nonetheless. In fact, inspired in part by Lawrence, quietly, without any coordination or even
mutual awareness, and wholly unnoticed politically, Orwell himself,
Thomas, Priestley, and a handful of others had been crafting the outline of just such an alternative philosophy through the 1930s. It was
this way of thinking that would come into its own in the war years
and the years immediately after. It was an approach that enabled them
to reject the crude choice between being pessimistic and optimistic,
radical and reactionary, bodily and intellectual, nationalist and in-
ternationalist. Most fundamentally of all, it was a philosophy that
turned its back once and for all on the notion that attaining social
improvement involved decrying the qualities of ordinary life itself.
Instead, it was in the ordinary that Orwell, Thomas, Priestley, and
others invested their hope. Their task wasn't to reach for the stars, to
reinvent the past, or to overthrow the social order. Rather, it was to
tell each and every one of us "to become *more* ourselves, not less."[67]

2

A Little Holding of Ground

I WROTE THE BULK OF this book not in Britain, but living in the suburb of Paddington, Sydney, Australia, in a sparkling summer, before the pandemic hit. I have a little attic writing room there, with a wooden desk at a window that looks out over a host of tin-roofed terrace houses, once workers' cottages, many now the homes of millionaires, climbing up a hillside otherwise covered in lush eucalyptus and Moreton Bay fig trees. There's a scar ripped through the trees and there's a constant rumbling of machinery from a large building site where some corporation has torn down a hospital and is building luxury retirement flats in its place. I remember well the first drafting of this very chapter. I had got a slight headache as I wrote; it's a hard business, and I was a bit anxious about the return of my daughter from her preschool soon, because I hadn't got enough written yet.

Nevertheless, I planned to knock off early and walk around the corner to the bakery for a break.

That was my everyday.

Nowadays, emanating from sociology, cultural studies, and anthropology departments across the world, there is a whole subliterature on the "everyday." One of those great paradoxes of contemporary academia is that much of it is utterly incomprehensible. For these scholars, everyday life is "the flow of social existence which is often routine and habitual, always embodied and temporal, often taken for granted and localized, and which for the most part changes incrementally but also sometimes dramatically."[1] There is some sense in descriptions like that when you take the time to work it out, and there are no doubt insights to be gleaned, but the gulf between the technical idiom and its subject is unsettlingly stark, and that leaves the study of the everyday politically inert today.

Much of this contemporary academic literature owes a strong debt to Marxism, and to the sense that although most people clearly value their everyday experiences, they might do so largely because they are suffering from "false consciousness." They are, in other words, celebrating the very things that keep them trapped in a social order that works against their interests. The French Marxist Henri Lefebvre stimulated this trend of thinking in the 1950s, probably the first time a serious and respected academic proposed the category of the "everyday" as a subject of enquiry. He argued that although people often felt there was an immense magic in everyday life that radical politicians and intellectuals often overlooked, this was often because they were simply the subject of distorting illusions "about themselves and their lack of power."[2]

There were none of these concerns about false consciousness in the work of George Orwell, Dylan Thomas, J. B. Priestley, or their colleagues. They wanted to be attentive to modern life afresh because they thought that there was something to discover there that others had missed, even perhaps the fundamental solution to Britain's ideological torpor. "Ordinary chaps that I meet everywhere, chaps I run across in pubs, bus drivers and travelling salesmen for hardware firms," Orwell had one of his fictional protagonists say, "can feel things cracking and collapsing under their feet."[3] If they knew what was wrong, perhaps they also possessed the answer to Britain's national woes, even if they were not fully aware of it.

The final few teasing pages of *Inside the Whale* set out the potential power of the everyday beautifully. What was needed for Britain's renewal would emerge not from "exploring the mechanisms of the mind" but rather from an "owning up to everyday facts and everyday emotions."[4] Once a thinker and a writer is able properly to explore everyday experiences, make sense of them, feel them, and report them back to a wide audience as evocatively as he or she can, then the spirit of social solidarity for which everyone—from T. S. Eliot and F. R. Leavis to W. H. Auden and Stephen Spender—had been longing for years might become possible again, Orwell explained. For millions of people, there could be something transformative in just reading these accounts:

> Here is a whole world of stuff which you have lived with since childhood, stuff which you supposed to be of its nature incommunicable, and somebody has managed to communicate it. The effect is to break down, at any rate momentarily, the solitude in which human beings live. . . . You feel the peculiar relief that comes not so much from understanding as from *being understood*. It is as though you could hear a voice speaking to you . . . with no humbug in it, no moral purpose, merely an implicit assumption that we are all alike.[5]

The primary challenge as Orwell saw it in 1939 was therefore to identify the people who would actually be able to do this work. Who was going to take the time to dive into the lived experience of people all around them, to tease out its essence, to share that essence with their fellow citizens in poetry, prose, or painting and help to build a new, shared story that could bind people together in enriching community as a result? He was clear that it wouldn't be the conventional intellectuals, but who else could it be?

The answer, of course, was all around him. Orwell knew that he had begun that work himself in the previous decade through essays, articles, and parts of his novels, especially the brilliant *Coming Up for Air*. *Inside the Whale* was partly an invitation for others to celebrate his achievement and to grasp its ideological importance. But what he seemed less aware of was that he had also been joined by a new generation of thinkers, who although often working in different genres and writing in different idioms shared the same fundamental insight. It was Orwell's insufferable intellectual ego that severed him personally from these potential colleagues and blinded him to their similarities in outlook—he looked down on Priestley for his pot-boiler popular novels and seemed entirely unaware of Thomas, even when he was briefly his boss at the BBC—but they existed nonetheless. And the work that they collectively shaped in the 1930s would provide the foundation for the soaring achievements of wartime cultural production that provide the subject for this book. The task of this chapter is to introduce the fundamental insights that drew these otherwise most unlikely comrades together.

The idea that the answers to Britain's woes were to be found in the everyday experiences of ordinary people, rather than in the grandeur of the country's vaunted traditions or in the pursuit of a revolution in economic and social order, was breathtakingly countercultural in the 1930s. The vast majority of socialist intellectuals at the time had no interest in real life. Their stated goal was to step back from the particular, the local, and the here-and-now and instead grasp the complexities of the "system," so that change of a magnitude not seen since the Industrial Revolution could come into view. Culturally conservative thinkers like Leavis were more tempted to peer into the everyday lives of ordinary people, partly because they felt that this was a world of which they had no direct experience. But they were constantly depressed by what they saw. "Looking across the gulf" from their lives to the lives of others, as the literary scholar John Carey puts it, "it seemed that the masses were not merely degraded and threatening, but not fully alive."[6]

As with most things, it was D. H. Lawrence who led the way to something better. Like most of his contemporaries, Lawrence had his moments of elitist disdain. He was eager to say that he thought the vast majority of people had been corrupted in the industrial era. "Men turn against heroic appeal, with a sort of venom," he wrote in his last major work, *Apocalypse*. They "listen to the call of mediocrity, wielding the insentient bullying power of mediocrity. . . . Hence the success of painfully inferior and base politicians."[7] But in general, he was nowhere near as crudely dismissive of the potential that lurked in the everyday as his peers. In part, this was because unlike Eliot, Leavis, and the others, he absolved the vast majority of individuals of the blame for the situation in which they found themselves. It was industrialism, capitalism, and the corruption of elites that had despoiled the country, not individual caprice. But there was also something deeper in his observations too, something that later provided the building blocks for an alternative.

In his wonderful essay "Insouciance," first published in 1928, Lawrence told of a meeting with two elderly ladies in a hotel. He had been looking out of his window at two men mowing the lawn. He had been considering their technique, feeling their efforts, pondering their relationship with each other and the natural world around them. Then, the ladies tried to draw him into a conversation about Benito Mussolini and the potential threat he posed to the world. The response Lawrence recalled to the ladies' seemingly innocent effort at polite political conversation was among the most revealing passages in his whole opus:

The worst ogress couldn't have treated me more villainously. I don't care about right and wrong, politics, Fascism, abstract liberty or anything else of the sort. I want to look at the mowers, and wonder why fatness, elderliness and black trousers should inevitably wear a new straw hat of the boater variety, move in stiff jerks, shove the end of the scythe-stroke with a certain violence, and win my hearty disapproval, as contrasted with young long thinness, bright blue cotton trousers, a bare black head and pretty lifting movement at the end of the scythe-stroke.[8]

Whereas some might put such a response down to an early-morning grump or a general unwillingness to be in company, Lawrence didn't leave the thought there. For him, this small interaction revealed something fundamental. "There simply is a deadly breach between actual living and this abstract caring," he said, continuing,

> What is actual living? It is a question mostly of direct contact. There was a direct sensuous contact between me, the lake, mountains, cherry trees, mowers, and a certain invisible but noisy chaffinch in a clipped lime tree. All this was cut off by the fatal shears of the abstract word Fascism, and the little old lady next door was the Atropos who cut the thread of my actual life this afternoon. She beheaded me, and flung my head into abstract space.[9]

Almost everything that would later matter in the vision that animates this book was here in this essay from Lawrence: the positive power of particularity, experience, place, nature, unpredictability, sentiment, and the dangers of politics as normally conceived by intellectuals, with all of its abstract principle, grand theorizing, and timeless, agencyless, system-based, distanced thinking. It reads like a conceptual table of contents. But despite his prescience, Lawrence couldn't quite create what he longed for. A public philosophy that truly spoke to the transformative potential of the everyday rather than the grand and the abstract just seemed out of reach. It was as if the well of social experience was fatally poisoned.

One of the most heartbreaking of his short essays, "Dull London," published in the same year as "Insouciance," revealed that fact. Here, Lawrence recounted how, however hard he tried, he could find no spiritual uplift, no shared sensation, no magic on the ordinary streets of England's capital. "All adventure seems to me crushed out of London," he wrote. "The traffic is too heavy! It used to be going somewhere, on an adventure. Now it only rolls massively and overwhelmingly, going nowhere, only dully and enormously *going*." Even the very noise of the city, which had once promised such potential for joy and excitement, now alienated him: "It booms like monotonous, far-off guns, in a monotony of crushing something, crushing the earth, crushing out life, crushing everything dead."[10]

This Lawrence felt more like the Eliot of *The Waste Land* than any optimistic alternative. It is why, when we look back now, it seems hard to imagine Lawrence as the creator of the optimistic, inclusive, generative political vision of those stories of St. Paul's and Britain's renewal in the Second World War that bewitched me in my bed as a child. Nonetheless, Lawrence had shown the way. He hadn't only asked the right questions, he had given a glimpse of what was possible. It was for the next generation to pick up where "Insouciance" and his other, more positive works had left off.

Orwell's efforts to rise to the challenge Lawrence set were present in all of his writing before the Second World War. The undercover reportage of *Down and Out in Paris and London*, the travelogue *The Road to Wigan Pier*, and the stories of mundane London life in *Keep the Aspidistra Flying* can all be read in this spirit. They were journeys of discovery into the parts of life into which his contemporaries had not looked for beauty, ideals, or hope. But it was his novel *Coming Up for Air*, written in 1938 as he recovered from his own tribulations in the Spanish Civil War and just a year before he began piecing together the intellectual analysis for *Inside the Whale*, that provided his most powerful attempt to explore the potential power of the everyday to change the course of British political life.

The very first line of the novel betrays its purpose. "The idea really came to me the day I got my new false teeth," Orwell had his protagonist, George Bowling, a forty-five-year-old middle-class man from outer London, declare.[11] And there it is: the confluence of the most unremarkable, mundane, ordinary occurrence—the arrival of the false teeth—and the seeming grandeur of a moment of intellectual creation—the birth of an idea. From then on, the novel moves deeper into the terrain marked out by Lawrence.

Coming Up for Air is, as the title suggests, a novel of escape. It is the story of a man desperate to get away both from the immediate circumstances of his life—wife, children, job, mortgage, the duties of work—and from the horrors besetting the broader world—rising international tensions, extremist politicians, irresponsible intellectuals fomenting further conflict. But it is also a novel of immersion. For Bowling's escape is not a grand one. His is a longing to return to a quieter time and to a place that allows for gentle contemplation. Get away from the big ideas, the noise, the ambition, Bowling is telling himself. Find somewhere where you can really focus on what is going on around you, just as Lawrence was at the beginning of "Insouciance."

As a result, Bowling makes a secret journey to the village of his childhood, Lower Binfield, to find quiet and solace and to fish in the pool. "Why don't people, instead of the idiocies they do spend their time on, just walk round *looking* at things?" Orwell has Bowling think to himself when he finally gets to the village. "That pond, for instance—all the stuff that's in it. Newts, water-snails, water-beetles, caddis-flies, leeches, and God knows how many other things that you can only see with a microscope. The mystery of their lives, down there under the water. You could spend a lifetime watching them, ten lifetimes, and still you wouldn't have got to the end of that one pool."[12] This is the spiritual heart of the novel. Calmness, and the benefits that come from it, is the whole point. "Stop firing that machine-gun! Stop chasing whatever you're chasing! Calm down, get your breath back, let a bit of peace seep into your bones," Bowling insists. "I only want to be alive. And I was alive at that moment when I stood looking at the primroses and the red embers under the hedge. It's a feeling inside you, a kind of peaceful feeling, and yet it's like a flame."[13]

These are beautiful passages, and it is no surprise that they sparked huge enthusiasm from Orwell's many literary devotees. The pursuit of calmness through reflection on the mundane became widely associated with Orwell. It was the fundamental idea that E. M Forster most admired in him; the idea that he thought was at the core of his political philosophy. "If a man cannot enjoy the return of spring, why should he be happy with a Labour-saving Utopia? . . . By retaining one's childhood love of such things as trees, fishes, butterflies and toads, one makes a peaceful and decent future a little more probable."[14]

Sadly, though, this is an overstatement. For much as he might have wanted to, in the 1930s at least, Orwell always held back from prosecuting the idea to its fullest. We can see that by the fact that throughout *Coming Up for Air*, Orwell ruthlessly undercut the worth of this very same vision. Bowling is wracked with doubt throughout his journey. At various moments, it all seems impossible, hopeless, undermined by the hostility of others, including his own wife and children, who ruthlessly mock their father's interest in fishing. Lower Binfield also lay bespoiled by the forces Orwell always despised. Thoughtless profit-motivated capitalist developers, on the one hand, have encroached into the countryside with their factories and housing developments. On the other, the precious, do-gooding self-satisfied preservers of nature and conventional beauty whom Orwell associated with the socialist intelligentsia had parcelled off other bits of land for their own exclusive leisure pursuits. On his disappointed return to London, moreover, Bowling finds himself at a political lecture by a virulent anti-Fascist campaigner who is desperate to haul Britain right back into another global war. He ends convinced that his effort to slow down the pace of life—to come up for air—will always come to nothing. "No use. We don't do it. Just keep on with the same bloody fooleries."[15]

Orwell's unwillingness to give succour to his character's aspirations to find sustainable uplift in the otherwise unremarkable was reflected throughout his writings in the mid- to late 1930s. Indeed, his work sometimes reads as if, just like George Bowling, he desperately wanted to believe that there could be something magical and transformative in the otherwise mundane, but he couldn't make himself hold on to the belief for long enough for the transformative moment ever to occur. This was in part, of course, just a sign that he had imbibed the pessimism of the age from Lawrence and others. It also, though, reflected his status as a perpetual outsider. Orwell was, after all, an author, writing under a pseudonym, who always tried to stay distant from his peers so that he could criticize their work. He was also a social commentator from a privileged background who did not always enjoy material success and yet never felt at home with those who endured poverty either.

This distance showed constantly in his descriptions of ordinary British life, even in texts where he was trying to evoke sympathy or even admiration. "It is a rather restless, cultureless life, centering round tinned food, *Picture Post*, the radio and the internal combustion engine," he summarized in *Road to Wigan Pier*. Working people lived with "the frightful debauchery of taste that has already been effected by a century of mechanization," he continued in language that couldn't have pleased F. R. Leavis more had it been copied straight out of the pages of *Scrutiny*. "This is almost too obvious and generally admitted to need pointing out," he continued. "But as a single instance, take taste in the narrowest sense—the taste for decent food. . . . Thanks to tinned food, cold storage, synthetic flavouring matters, etc., the palate is almost a dead organ." "In a healthy world there would be no demand for tinned foods, aspirins, gramophones, gaspipe chairs, machine guns, daily newspapers, telephones, motor-cars," he continued gravely to lecture, listing a host of the diversions that ordinary people actually enjoyed.[16]

Orwell's own unwillingness to prosecute what we might call the case for the everyday with full vigour explains his sense in *Inside the Whale* that nobody in Britain had yet done so, especially when combined with his general sense of intellectual superiority over his peers. But it is still not an obviously correct interpretation of the full range of work available in the 1930s. For others were trying, as he would have seen had he looked just a little harder.

Most prominent among those others, at least in the sense of public profile, was J. B Priestley. Priestley had one powerful advantage over Orwell when he wrote of the suburbs, the provincial towns, and the ordinary working- and middle-class communities of 1930s England: that was where he was from. Brought up in the West Riding of Yorkshire, the son of a schoolteacher, Priestley drew throughout his career on the people he met as a young boy and the experiences he had of a very ordinary, undistinguished childhood.[17] "There are moments even now," he wrote as an elderly man, "when I find myself in some country lane . . . forgetting how the years have gone and that I am now a heavy ageing man. But before the tide of regret sweeps over my mind, the grey and salty tide, there sparkles, like some treasure on the sand, not some mere memory of past pleasure, but, for a flashing quarter-second, the old delight itself."[18]

A scholarship to Cambridge University propelled Priestley from this world to a very different one, and his early career after Cambridge was spent writing unremarkable but extremely popular novels, including *The Good Companions* and *Angel Pavement,* which were among the very best sellers of the age. In literary circles, this work was of little note; reviews in the likes of *Scrutiny* were sneering, to the extent that Priestley was occasionally marked out as an example of Britain's intellectual decline. But one of the reasons for the mass appeal of Priestley's novels was that they displayed an unusual degree of attention to the small details of provincial and city life, a characteristic that would also stand Priestley in good stead in later years as a chronicler of everyday experience.

The work that ensured more serious attention, however, was not a novel at all but a travelogue, *English Journey*. Like Orwell's more celebrated equivalent, *The Road to Wigan Pier*, which it predated by three years, *English Journey* was an effort to grasp what was really happening to ordinary English people, their communities, aspirations, families, schools, workplaces, and daily lives, as they faced the strains of the Depression. "I am here, in a time of stress, to look at the face of England, however blank or bleak that face may chance appear, and to report truthfully what I see there," Priestley announced. And what he found was that the people were the strongest part of England, whatever orthodox intellectual opinion might say. "Bernard Shaw once declared that all he wanted to do was to abolish the working-class and put in its place some sensible people," Priestley explained, but having toured the country in a way that London's politicians and intellectuals rarely brought themselves to do, he would rather see it populated as it currently is than "by average members of the Fabian Society."[19]

Powerful though this vote of confidence in the English people was, the reasons for Priestley's faith were not particularly clearly stated in *English Journey*. There was little here of the philosophizing of Lawrence or even Orwell, no emphasis on the connection people found between each other and the places they lived, or on their ability to avoid the grandiose abstractions that addled the brains of those who lived for politics. Instead, Priestley provided a series of generalizations about the character of the people he met and the way in which it compared with those in more privileged parts of society. In part this came down to resilience. "Such men as these," he said of those working in onerous occupations or in precarious employment, staring the real possibility of poverty in the face, "stand on their own two feet, do their jobs with a will, stoutly resist stupid opposition but give way to affection." They "are grand lumps of character. What—in the name of everything but supermen—more can you want?"[20] It was also, in part, a claim about kindness. There is a natural "courtesy of the ordinary English people," he reported. "I have noticed more downright rudeness and selfishness in one night in the stalls of a West End theatre than I have observed in the streets of some dirty manufacturing town, where you would have thought everybody would be hopelessly brutalized."[21]

Vague as these generalizations might have been, they acted nonetheless as an important corrective to the intellectual tendencies of his time, whether in the form of the brutal pessimism of an Eliot or a Leavis or the self-satisfaction and smug dismissal of the intellect of actual working people, as opposed to an imagined proletariat, that came from an Auden or Spender.

In that light, *English Journey*'s most powerful contribution was its defence of suburbia and the new towns, those parts of the country that had received the most withering contempt from the vast majority of Priestley's contemporaries. Priestley described with warmth "the England of arterial and by-pass roads, of filling stations and factories that look like exhibition buildings, of giant cinemas and dance-halls and cafes, bungalows with tiny garages, cocktail bars, Woolworths, motor-coaches, wireless, hiking, factory girls looking like actresses, greyhound racing and dirt tracks, swimming pools"; precisely the part of England that Orwell had George Bowling trying to escape.[22] Moreover, Priestley's defence of this part of the country was far subtler than most of the argumentation in *English Journey*. He argued, for example, that although the suburbs often looked standardized, in Leavis's terms, or as if copied from a template, they nonetheless exhibited real individuality if one bothered to look closely enough. Of the main arterial road in Swindon, for example, he wrote that it was "lined on each side by tiny semi-detached houses of red brick. There were a great many of them and they were all alike, *except* in their little front

gardens. Some house-holders favoured dahlias and Michaelmas dai-
sies, others preferred the bright geranium. All these gardens, though
hardly bigger than a tablecloth, were flowering profusely."[23]

It was from this defence of the suburbs that an argument most
clearly approaching a public philosophy emerged in *English Journey*.
This part of England, Priestley insisted, was "essentially democratic."
It was an "England at last without privilege."[24] What looked like
empty, soulless standardization to Leavis or his like was, in fact, the
harbinger of something exciting and something new. It was an England
without the distinctions of class, without an aristocracy, without an
anxiety about the old and the new. England was being reborn, bringing
a combination of the qualities that had always been best in the nation and the qualities needed for the twentieth century. It was here,
among the people of the suburbs, that Priestley found real hope for
the future:

> I remember younger folk . . . all products of this newest England,
> and I saw that there is a section of people who have its strength
> but are untouched by its weakness. I met them all over the
> country, not many at a time, for there are not enough of them
> to make a crowd in any one place. . . . They are not prigs, though
> being young and earnest they are inclined at times to be a shade
> too solemn. They are not saving their souls or going about doing
> good. But they have a social consciousness; their imagination is
> not blunted; they know that we are interdependent and that
> bluffing and cheating are useless. . . . They are good citizens and
> as yet we have no city worthy of them.[25]

Passages like this gave a powerful glimpse of what was to come in
later years: a truly democratic mode of thinking, confident, optimistic,
yet also grounded in an unblinkered awareness of social reality. The
very last phrase though—the sense that "as yet we have no city worthy
of them"—also revealed that the Priestley of the 1930s was not yet

fully convinced of his own story. Just like Orwell, that is, he still instinctively struggled with much of the modern. For all of his desire to paint an inspiring picture of the potential of a new country, *English Journey* remained unconvinced by many of the same characteristics as his peers had been.

This was revealed most starkly in his description of two English towns: Blackpool and Birmingham. Priestley was unrelenting in his dismissal of both. Blackpool, of course, had been looked down on by social commentators and reformers for generations as a town where the working class headed for leisure and ended up indulging in vice. But Priestley was certain that the twentieth-century version was far worse than anything that had come before. "The Blackpool that sang about Charlie Brown and the girl with curly curls [in the nineteenth century] was the Mecca of a vulgar but alert and virile democracy," he said. But "I am not sure about the new Blackpool." "It has developed a pitiful sophistication—machine-made and not really English— that is much worse than the old hearty vulgarity," he felt. And it was a situation made worse, he believed, by the local entertainers' fondness for "weary negroid ditties" from the United States.[26]

Of Birmingham he was, if anything, even more biting: "I loathed the whole long array of shops, with their nasty bits of meat, their cough mixtures, their *Racing Specials,* their sticky cheap furniture, their shoddy clothes, their fly-brown pastry, their coupons and sales and lies and dreariness and ugliness," he intoned.[27] Ending with that term "ugly" was no accident, of course. It would have reminded his contemporaries of D. H. Lawrence, who frequently dismissed the towns of industrial England in exactly the same way.

Also, like Lawrence, of course, Priestley exempted the vast majority of people themselves from the blame of even the worst parts of popular culture. People turned to the tawdry, the cheap, and the easy, he believed, because of the pressures of their own lives. Those living constantly on the edge of despair cannot be blamed for failing to resist the siren "calls of either the confectionary drama of the films or a few

quick drinks," he acknowledged.[28] But the critique remained nonetheless, and at times it threatened to derail his entire project. "I do
not feel that any of the activities in this new England" can provide
the really solid basis for a new culture, he wrote towards the end of
his text.[29] In fact, so awful did he find much of them that it became
hard to decide "whether the people were better off or worse off in the
nineteenth-century England" than they were in the democratic new.
This kind of ambivalence similarly flowed through the Mass Observation movement that took its early inspiration from Priestley.[30]

This is how Priestley's thought ended in the 1930s as war beckoned.
Echoing Lawrence, once again, he worried that whereas the Victorians "had found a green and pleasant land," they and their succes-
sors "had left a wilderness of dirty bricks." England now "had blackened fields, poisoned rivers, ravaged the earth, and sown filth and
ugliness with a lavish hand." Often, "what you see looks like a debauchery of cynical greed."[31] We had sunk "down into the dark bog
of greedy industrialism, where money and machines are of more importance than men and women." Unlike some, he hadn't given up
on a more optimistic ending, but it would not come easily. "It is for
us to find the way out again, into the sunlight."[32]

Unbeknownst to either Orwell or Priestley in 1939, of course, that
"way out" would be discovered during the war itself, drawn partly by
their own hands. But even before that, and also apparently without
them being aware, its fundamentals were already being chartered by
a cultural peer of theirs to whom neither often gave a second thought
in the 1930s, Dylan Thomas.

Thomas was a son of the suburbs, just as Priestley had been. But
unlike Priestley, he did not have his Cambridge moment to wrench
him out of his hometown and into the cultural establishment. He
didn't have time in the trenches, either, or in the British imperial
army or on the battlefields of Spain, as so many of his generation did.
All the young Thomas ever had was Swansea, or more specifically Up-

lands and Cwmdonkin Drive, the street on which he spent his youth. All of this meant that his artistic points of reference were primarily the other children he played with at school, which he left aged just fifteen, and the adults they became. His greatest political influences were Bert Trick, the local grocer, who was an avid reader of the new philosophies of the Left; the local newspaper from which he thought he could earn a living; and the debates and arguments of the politically engaged people of his Labour-voting town, which focused at least as much on the personal rivalries of the street and the local council as on the major issues of the age. The grandest aspects of his thinking came from the wonderful books his dad brought into the house—all the classics that captivated a "self-improving" Welshman of his age—and, of course, from the undisputed genius he had for seeing it all and capturing it in words, a genius that was apparent long before he had even turned twenty.[33]

For many at the time, this provincial background entailed that Thomas could never be a properly political thinker. Despite the acknowledged brilliance of his poetry, and the number of important patrons his work and charisma provided him from the mid-1930s onwards, Thomas barely registered as a "public intellectual" in the Depression years. Insofar as he was discussed in conventionally intellectual circles, he was cast as a distinctly antipolitical thinker, someone keen only to incite "revolt against the political poetry" of Auden, Spender, and colleagues and turn his art instead back to "magic, religion, guilt or a world of personal relations."[34]

This view dominates today too. There is almost no serious scholarship on Thomas as a political thinker, no effort to understand the origins or impact of his work on the nation's ideology. Instead, academics tend to render his wartime writings—where he very explicitly painted a vision of the Britain for which he craved—as the exception to an antipolitical rule.

But this is entirely misconceived, as Thomas himself was often at pains to point out. Thomas described himself as "a socialist . . . , though a very unconventional one."[35] "Don't imagine the great jawed writer brooding over his latest masterpiece in the oak study," he wrote to his first lover, Pamela Hansford Johnson, before they had met, "but a thin curly little person, smoking too many cigarettes, with a crocked lung, and writing his vague verses in the back room of a provincial villa."[36] And there it all was. Through poetry and prose, in the 1930s, and later in radio essays and in his triumphant play for voices, *Under Milk Wood*, Thomas gave a distinctly political voice, dignity, and power to people in their everyday settings. He just couldn't help it.

Even as a very young man, Thomas was aware that his ability to capture his world in words had the potential to be of very great public and political import. When Priestley published *English Journey*, to much acclaim in 1934, Thomas became desperate to produce an alternative, a "Welsh Journey." Nicknaming Priestley the "Bad Companion," he mocked what he took to be Priestley's unpersuasive concern with everyday life.[37] His travelogue would owe nothing to Priestley's "method of approach," he said. Instead it would be "far more personal and intimate," resulting in "an intimate chronicle of my personal journey among people and places."[38]

Thomas never managed to write his "Welsh Journey." No publisher was willing to come forward with the kind of advance that would have attracted him, and even if they had done so, the likelihood is that he would have spent the advance long before he had set out on his travels. Completing a project of this kind required the kind of discipline that Thomas never had. But he conducted the work in another way instead, writing long, perceptive letters to his friends and to those he admired, penning short stories and essays for the newspapers, and feeding his reflections into his ever more sophisticated and successful poetry.

Even in the very earliest of these writings, Thomas's worldview was clear. There was no merit in grandeur or abstraction; nothing to be gained by theorizing about "the system," as Auden and Spender had, or "lost tradition," like Eliot and Leavis. Everything worth finding, discussing, working out, and building on was to be found in the everyday. Writing to Pamela Hansford Johnson in 1934 of his neighbours on Swansea's Cwmdonkin Drive, Thomas said that even on the days when he found them "dreadful"—when he was most keenly alert to "all their little horrors"—he found it impossible to see them "as the pitiable products of the capitalist system, as wage-slaves, economic eunuchs, mass-systemized, the capitally-lettered Workers," as most of his socialist contemporaries would have urged him to do. "They're not," Thomas insisted. "They're people, from a particular place, with particular personalities, and each of them is worth considering on his or her own merits."[39]

In part this came from Thomas's literary sensibilities. He hated abstraction and he loved specificity. But there was always a profound argument lurking here too, one that would shape his politics throughout his life. "I thought of a definition of beauty," he wrote in 1933. "Like all such definitions, it is too limited," but it was worth stating anyway. Beauty is "acquaintance plus wonder."[40] That would be the core of his thinking for the next two decades, and not just when it came to beauty. All that we truly value in our lives together, Thomas believed—including the great vaunted political ideals of community, freedom, and nationhood—aren't to be found in grand places or in imaginary utopias or in bold philosophical speculation. They're actually to be found lurking in the everyday, waiting to be discovered by people willing to look for them and capable of seeing them with all of the sense of wonder that they deserve. To Thomas, nothing mattered more than the light in the eyes of someone who had found magic nestled in the midst of something others dismiss as entirely mundane.

It was this juxtaposition of the magical and the everyday that was Thomas's major contribution to the political movement that this book is all about. What Britain required if it was ever to escape its age of torpor was a capacity for wonder in normal life. This idea was fundamental. It would echo through everything that came later. The films, plays, poetry, prose, and photography of wartime, all of them were driven by this central insight. It also, of course, marked a radical break with the pessimism that had remained from Lawrence. Whereas Orwell and Priestley continued to gloom about the ugliness of contemporary life, for example, the youthful Thomas wrote, "There is nothing on God's earth that is, in itself, an ugly thing"; it is merely "sickness of the mind" that makes it so. Nothing "is ugly except what I make ugly, and the lowest and the highest are level to the eyes of the air."[41]

Thomas's early writing was captivated by his efforts to demonstrate the truth of this contention. His early letters, prose, and poetry were full of increasingly brilliant descriptions of the magic to be found in everyday life, from the "tiny, scarlet ants that crawl from the holes in the rock to my busy hand" to the shipwreck he could see from his window, with its "three broken masts, like three nails in the breast of a wooden Messiah."[42]

Most of all, Thomas turned again and again to memories of childhood to make his case. He would return there throughout his career, as we shall see in the chapters ahead, but these early efforts were among the most profound. Childhood, he knew, is that one moment in life where the separation of the grand from the small makes no sense to anyone. It is the time when the most magical aspects of existence can be—have to be—rendered out of the immediate environment around us.

Thomas, as a young adult, exerted all his creative energy to rediscover and redescribe just what this ability to use wonder to create brilliance from the mundane felt like. His early work is full of such efforts, all dazzlingly told. They are memories like this of a day holidaying on the sand: "'If it could only just, if it could only just?' your lips said again and again as you scooped, in the hob-hot sand, dungeons, garages, torture-chambers, train tunnels, arsenals, hangars for zeppelins, witches' kitchens, vampires' parlours, smugglers' cellars, trolls' grogshops, sewers, under a ponderous cracking castle. . . . Could donkeys go on the ice?"[43]

Brighton Beach, 1931–1936
Bill Brandt © Bill Brandt Archive

All of this meant that as war broke out—a global conflict of a scale unprecedented in human history—Thomas was clear what he needed to do: he had to write short stories about growing up in Swansea. Not for him, the excitement of defending Western civilization from the Nazis or the anxious intellectual analysis of Orwell's *Inside the Whale*. Instead, he was engrossed by *Portrait of the Artist as a Young*

Dog: "stories towards a provincial autobiography," as he called them. "They are all about Swansea life," he wrote to Bert Trick, reminding us again of "the pubs, clubs, billiard rooms, promenades, adolescence and the suburban nights."[44] And he was writing them because that's where he believed any real hope for the country must lie.

Portrait of the Artist as Young Dog has been paradoxically overlooked by literary scholars interested in Thomas's development as an artist, partly because its faux-Joycean title always made it seem like pastiche and partly because the stories are not as powerful or as evocative as some of those that were to come. But the book meant a lot to Thomas himself, and it allowed him to set the scene for all the material he would produce in wartime and the years after. Reading it today, it remains a breathtaking piece of advocacy for the fundamental importance of the utterly parochial in human affairs. "You've got a beautiful name," one of the youthful characters in the book tells another at one point. "Oh, it's just ordinary," she replies.[45] It's an exchange that renders Thomas's whole argument as clear as it is possible to be. If only we cared to look.

The immediate response to Thomas's argument was largely to ignore it. Among those who did not, it found few friends. The conservative-minded critics of *Scrutiny* could not stand it. In Thomas, "we have the fanatic preacher, childhood fear of death and the flesh-creeping bogey, terror in the suburbs of sordidness and drunken hysteria in the precincts of bars," *Scrutiny's* reviewer hissed in their review of *Portrait of the Artist as a Young Dog*.[46] It was pointless at best, dangerously sentimental at worse. And to the Left there seemed to be no politics in it at all, because there was no systemic analysis, no stepping back from the particular to see how the pieces fitted together into a theory of history or a macroecomomic whole.

It is true that Thomas's politics was not as clear in the 1930s as it would be in the 1940s and 1950s. His work wasn't in its final form before the conflict. Nonetheless, there *was* politics, and it was fairly

Evening in Kenwood, 1931–1936
Bill Brandt © Bill Brandt Archive

straightforward to discern. Ordinary people—the kind of people you'd meet in a lazy day in a Swansea park or a rowdy night in a pub—can do magical things, their everyday lives full of brilliance, and there can be no hope for any of us unless we remember that. Such a thought might sound straightforward, but it marked a major break from the primary tendencies of British thought since the First World War, tendencies that owed themselves to Lawrence. In so doing, it replaced the pessimism and harshness that had characterized most social reflection in the 1930s with an immense generosity. Thomas simply refused to see anything other than possibility in the everyday lives of those in front of him. He was happiest on the most crowded days in the most ordinary of settings, on a windswept Welsh beach, on the streets as workers strolled to work, jammed into a bus with all ages and all classes, sitting in the corner of the pub as people pressed to get to the bar.

Beyond that, the argument that Thomas was beginning to make was a call for change at a very deep level. The major building blocks of British thought had been conceived on a worldview that he was throwing away. What it meant to care about community, about freedom, and about nationhood was different when you started from where Thomas did in comparison with where Leavis or Eliot or Spender or Auden did. All of that would come into sharp relief in the Second World War. When people began to ask what they were fighting for, why they were putting themselves through this ordeal, then they were drawn back to those big, fundamental values. Thomas's job in the war, in which he would be joined by Orwell and by Priestley, but also by others like Barbara Jones, Bill Brandt, and Laurie Lee, was to encourage them to see those values from the starting point of the extraordinary power of everyday life and not from the perspective of the orthodox. Chapters 3, 4, and 5, about the war years and their aftermath, show how they did just that.

3

The Properties of
My Memory Remain

W<small>E BURIED MY DAD</small> on a hillside overlooking Cardiff, South
Wales, with a view that stretches to the Taff valley and Caerphilly
beyond, on a bright late spring afternoon in 2017. Our elderly neighbours, still known to me only as Mr. and Mrs. Hawkins, sat on folding
chairs by the graveside, as did my wife, Lizzy, with our squirming and
squealing two-year-old daughter, Freya, on her lap. Everyone else
stood, people from every part of my dad's life—colleagues, neighbours,
teachers, carers, taxi drivers—feeling the soft, dewy Welsh grass under
their feet, little bits of the moisture dampening the bottom of their
trousers. And together we looked out. We saw the crisscrossing roads,
the shops, and the schools and we heard the distant echoes of cars,
buses, tractors, and the occasional shout; everyone else going on about
their business. And we all remembered the times my dad had driven
along the same streets, the voices he had heard up close then, the
people he'd laughed with, and tears that he had shed.

There is a reason that people still read Dylan Thomas in Wales. The idea that he began to sketch in the late 1930s of the real meaning in life coming not from the grandiose but from the everyday, not from the cosmopolitan but from the parochial, was so very alive at that graveside that day. These fundamentals still lie deep within the psyche in parts of that community, making sense of the world, even at moments of immense personal pain, holding people together, reminding them of why that sense of community matters so much precisely when nothing else can be held in any coherent order. I doubt there was a person there who did not feel it in their bones. None of us could have articulated it quite as Thomas had done, of course, but that was his special gift.

Despite its enormous power, the vision that Thomas and his contemporaries created almost died as soon as it had been born. For there could not have been a worse time for it to emerge than in the years just before Britain descended once again into a world war. Indeed, there was something deeply ironic about a philosophy grounded in the unrealized potential of the everyday being crafted just as everyone's everyday was swallowed up by the most extraordinary challenge that the country had ever seen.

Even having lived through the immense disruptions of COVID-19, it is hard for us to recall now just how existential a threat the war seemed to pose to ordinary life in Britain, especially in its early years, or how vulnerable the very idea of the everyday had become.[1] We have become accustomed to the tales of a "people's war," those sometimes clichéd images of St. Paul's in the Blitz that my dad shared with me as a child, the stories of Dunkirk spirit, and the old newsreel films of people gathered around pianos while taking shelter from the bombs in the stations of the London Underground, singing along to their favourites from George Formby and Gracie Fields.[2] We also all know, of course, how it all turned out. But none of that was how it appeared as the conflict commenced. Instead, the buildup to and then the outbreak of the Second World War was a time of absolute terror for those at the centre of this book. Everything they cared about seemed to be about to collapse forever.

"The old life we're used to is being sawn off at the roots. I can feel it happening," George Orwell had his everyday hero, George Bowling, exclaim the year before Neville Chamberlain returned from Munich.[3] When the bombs started falling over Swansea, the contrast between the normal, mundane, but beautiful city that he adored and the horror of the violence became almost too much for Thomas to take. "I can't imagine Gower bombed," he wrote to his friend Vernon Watkins in the late summer of 1940. "High explosives at Pennard. Flaming onions over Pwlldu. And Union Street ashen. It is all too near." And it wasn't only Swansea, of course. "I had to go to London last week," he continued, and "the Hyde Park guns were booming. Guns on the top of Selfridges. A plane brought down in Tottenham Court Road. White-faced taxis still trembling through the streets."[4]

The destructive force of war did not only threaten Orwell's and Thomas's emerging worldview. It swiftly wiped out the ideals of their contemporaries. The rural romanticism that had dominated conservative thinking in the 1930s—what Orwell had dubbed the "the Olde Tea Shoppe" view of the world—quickly looked ridiculous.[5] Inspired by T. S. Eliot and F. R. Leavis, artists like John Piper and Graham Sutherland had once toured Britain to paint the romantic ruins of historic castles covered in ivy, but the only ruins that caught their imagination now were burnt-out buildings blown apart by Nazi bombs.[6] The orthodox socialism of the literary establishment of the Left fared little better. W. H. Auden infamously fled to the United States as soon as he could, capitalism not seeming that bad after all. Stephen Spender physically stayed, but intellectually he began his long journey away from his convictions of the 1930s. His new venture with Cyril Connolly, a magazine called *Horizon*, was launched the month that the war broke out and eschewed all of his former ideals. "The impetus given by Left Wing politics is for the time exhausted," its first editorial ran. "And however much we should like to have a paper that was revolutionary in opinions or original in technique, it is impossible to do so. . . . Our standards are aesthetic, and our politics are in abeyance."[7]

Despite all of these dangers, though, something truly spectacular occurred during the war. Orwell, Thomas, and J. B. Priestley did not follow Spender in abandoning their previous convictions. Instead, they deepened and enriched them. What had begun as a generalized reaction to the views of others and as a raw response to the experiences of the Depression became something far closer to a political creed, a set of values that made sense of what was going on. As it did, they attracted many new and celebrated names to the cause—Laurie Lee, Bill Brandt, and Barbara Jones among them—and the ideas began to sink into the mainstream, with politicians and bureaucrats becoming tantalizingly aware of their potential popular power.

None of this was conscious, planned, or organized, of course. That is not how these thinkers worked. They wrote independently from one another, rarely met, and when they did, they disliked each other. They certainly never set out intending to build a political movement. But their achievement was real, nonetheless. They provided Britain with a new way of understanding the fundamental concepts at the core of our political imagination—community, nationhood, freedom, and democracy—and they did it by refusing to see these concepts as grand abstractions. Instead, they grounded them in an account of the ordinary experiences of everyday life even as it was played out in the midst of the extraordinary context of war. Reinvigorating those ideas and that approach for our own age is the purpose of this book. It is the task of this chapter to understand how the work began in this most unlikely of times, especially when it came to the first of those notions, the idea of community.

The sense of togetherness, tenderness, the belief that we are better when we somehow stand together, was always at the core of the ideal. "The real objective," Orwell summarized in one of his occasional direct statements of political purpose, "is human brotherhood." "Men use up their lives in heart-breaking political struggles, or get themselves killed in civil wars, or tortured in secret prisons of the Gestapo," he continued, "not in order to establish some central-heated, air-conditioned, strip-lighted Paradise, but because they want a world in which human beings love each other instead of swindling and murdering one another."[8] "Seeking kinship with everything, daffodils, sheep, shoehorns, saints, bees," Thomas equally characteristically put it, "is exactly what I do."[9]

But where was this sense of community to be found as war threatened to rip the country apart? It couldn't come from militarism or from what Priestley called "an idiotic nationalism." Britain had tried that in the First World War and had never fully recovered.[10] "What English people of nearly all classes loathe from the bottom of their hearts is the swaggering officer type, the jingle of spurs and the crash of boots," Orwell insisted in his greatest wartime tract, *The Lion and the Unicorn*.[11] It couldn't come from a big, booming, noble idealism either. The words of D. H. Lawrence were still ringing in their ears. "Is love of humanity the same as real, warm, individual love?" Lawrence had asked. "Nonsense. It is the moonshine of our warm day, a hateful reflexion." Community had to be found in real, shared, everyday experience. "The actual living quick itself is alone the creative reality," Lawrence had instructed. "Once you abstract from this, once you generalize and postulate Universals, you have departed from creative reality, and entered the realm of static fixity, mechanism, materialism."[12]

What was required for a widespread sense of community, therefore, was a practical experience of each other immediately together, a sense of joy in people's company, whether developed through play, collaboration, love, competition, or some other shared endeavour. It had to be concrete. It had to be real. It had to draw from the extraordinary power of the everyday. But that is precisely why it was so difficult to imagine achieving it during a time of war. War drove people apart either by the immediate reality of violence or by the equally real terror of what violence might bring either to oneself or to one's loved ones. Orwell, Priestley, Thomas, and others were faced with what seemed an almost impossible situation. As the political theorist Bonnie Honig has more recently put it, they were craving "the capacity for concern absent nearly all its necessary conditions."[13]

As war broke out, this anxiety was captured most perfectly in an initially surprising place, the last novel of Virginia Woolf, *Between the Acts*. Woolf had failed to capture the attention of any of the writers at the centre of this book or to touch sympathetically on any of their themes. Orwell dismissed her as interested only in "technical innovation" rather than in "any moral meaning or political implication," and in typically conceited style he left it at that.[14] But in fact, Woolf's earlier work had been even more starkly opposed to his than he had taken the time to notice.

Woolf was always drawn towards the idea of capturing everyday reality in prose, just as Orwell, Priestley, and Thomas had tried to do. If you are interested in thinking about what fiction ought to do, she had once said, then you need to "imagine an ordinary mind on an ordinary day." But she nonetheless starkly disagreed with Orwell and colleagues as to what such an ordinary day might look like. She had no time for the notion that there is some kind of communal harmony underlying everyday life just waiting to be discovered and celebrated, as suggested in *English Journey, Coming Up for Air,* or *Portrait of the Artist as a Young Dog.* Instead, her work rippled with the opposite idea, familiar to readers of Eliot's *Waste Land,* that modern life was discordant to its very core. Every day in modern life, she insisted, the "mind receives a myriad impressions—trivial, fantastic, evanescent, or engraved with the sharpness of steel. From all sides they come, an incessant shower of innumerable atoms."[15] The task of literature was to respond to that disharmony and to avoid imposing on it any illusory and conventional generic order.

Between the Acts, however, was different, or at least it was at first sight.[16] Here, Woolf seemed to be compelled to discover whether a very conventional kind of community life could be both experienced and described in England at the very point when, in the words of her husband, Leonard Woolf, the barbarians were at the gates. The novel tells of an extended family group gathered in a small stately home called Pointz Hall putting on a historic pageant for the entertainment of the whole community, as they have done every year for the last seven years, under the direction of an eccentric outsider by the name of Miss La Trobe. There is nothing grand about the pageant, though, or the preparations for it. Instead, it is the very conventional habits, everyday rituals, and common practices of a normal collection of English people, Woolf appears to suggest, that offer us the chance to keep even the worst horrors of destructive violence at bay.

Everything is held together at Pointz Hall and in the neighbouring town by the parochial and the known. The novel beautifully displays the contrasting speeds of the life of everyday harmony and that of violence and destruction. Whereas war races towards us, and power insists always that things be done and done now, time in this small English community seems both slow and long. Unremarkable rituals are repeated across generations. They have existed for so long, in fact, that people cannot remember when they started. There is time in such a community for doing nothing, for sitting together, relaxing in each other's company, thinking about little more than the fairy tales that are told to children, or the romances of adolescence, or the everyday miscellanea of country life. There is no hurry. The only forces that rush are those that propel us to destruction.

In painting this picture, Woolf expertly displayed the powerful conventionalism of everyday speech. There is repetition and rhythm to discussions about preparing for lunch, picnicking, worrying about the weather, being grumpy that the county council has done nothing about the water supply, putting on a play, and, of course, taking tea together. "The noise of china and chatter drowned her murmur. 'Sugar for you?' they were saying. 'Just a spot of milk? And you?' 'Tea without milk or sugar. That's the way I like it.' 'A bit too strong? Let me add water.'"[17] Everyone, no matter how rich or poor, young or old, can find their place in conversations like these, Woolf appears to suggest. Their lack of complication, even emptiness, presents a warmth, a familiarity, and even a sense of equality between the classes that provides a real opportunity for sentimental attachment to emerge between people who otherwise might not have very much to do with each other.

In places, *Between the Acts* even reminds us of D. H. Lawrence's essay "Insouciance" by dismissing those who seek to bring matters of so-called grander import into view. Just as Lawrence in his essay railed against the two women who sought to get him to think about Fascism rather than lawn mowing, so Woolf's novel dismisses the one character, Giles Oliver, who tries to get people to direct their attention to the world stage. As others take tea, worry about the quality of the cakes, and concern themselves with who should sit where, Oliver frets about the oncoming war and the economy. He is roundly dismissed for taking up "a pose." His wife looks on and decides that she does not admire him for his seriousness but dismisses him as a "silly little boy."[18]

Woolf, though, was no convert to the worldview of Orwell, Priestley, and Thomas. For as *Between the Acts* proceeds, it becomes ever clearer that none of this will be strong enough to hold the community together for long. Violence lurks everywhere in *Between the Acts*, not only the violence of the oncoming war but also the violence that Woolf still believed sits beneath the surface of all human relationships. It pops up between the cracks all the time, whether in the form of newspaper reports of a horrific rape of a young girl by British soldiers, the reminiscences of an old solider terrifying a child, the intense enmity of a couple constantly falling in and out of love, or the mindless act of crushing a snake and a toad under one's foot in the grass.

There is another, more worrying, kind of violence in *Between the Acts* too: the violence of power in a community that without it constantly threatens to descend into chaos. The communal togetherness with which the novel begins, that is, is latterly revealed to be only an illusion. It is only through aggressive assertions of an individual will that the collective togetherness can actually be experienced. This is displayed most insistently by the person of Miss La Trobe and her dictatorial control over the play and her audience. Without her no one knows what to do. The audience of the play are shown continuously looking at the programme that La Trobe has provided for guidance as to where they are meant to be and when and how they are supposed to respond to what they have been shown. They have no ability to shape their own behaviour. Indeed, their collective identity as "an audience" is the result of their subjection to the power of the director.[19]

All of this is displayed at its most terrifying as the play ends. At this point, Miss La Trobe has children from the village hold up mirrors, tin cans, shining candlesticks, old jars, anything that reflects, so that the audience can see themselves on stage. The result is pandemonium:

What's the notion? Anything that's bright enough to reflect, presumably, ourselves?

Ourselves! Ourselves!

Out they leapt, jerked, skipped. Flashing, dazzling, dancing, jumping. Now old Bart . . . he was caught. Now Manresa. Here a nose . . . There a skirt . . . Then trousers only . . . Now perhaps a face . . . Ourselves? But that's cruel. To snap us as we are, before we've had time to assume . . . And only, too, in parts . . . That's what's so upsetting and utterly unfair.[20]

Horrified by what they have seen, the audience realize that the all of what Woolf called the "one-making" was an illusion.[21] There is no natural harmony, there is no deep attachment between them. They are, in reality, "in parts." As the story continues, we see the audience members desperately hoping for everything to settle back down into its rhythm and routine, its soothing familiarity and harmony. They want nothing more than for the play to end on a reassuring note. But they are disappointed. No moment of reunification comes. Instead, the play concludes with a gramophone plaintively playing the fundamental message Miss La Trobe has for them all: "Dispersed are we; who have come together. . . . Dispersed are we."[22]

This fear of dispersal wracked millions as the Second World War began. Even if they did not share Woolf's modernist aesthetic and believe that life was inevitably discordant in the twentieth century or hold, like Eliot, Lawrence, and Leavis, that industrialism had torn the heart out of the "organic community," they knew now that something big was at stake. What if everything valuable in life really was about to fall apart? What if everyone was about to be wrenched out of their daily routines, stripped of everything that provided stability, security, and a sense of solidarity one to another, overnight? They were "terrified," as Priestley put it, "by the thought that it might be the worst . . . ever imagined, or, indeed, something unimaginable; a numbing horror."[23]

To some, escape seemed like the only possibility. Human community, indeed love itself, might only continue to be found in the spaces where the war was not. It was this thought that propelled Thomas's desperate efforts to avoid being called up for active service. "What do I want for Christmas?" he rhetorically asked Vernon Watkins in December 1939. "I want a war-escaper—a sort of ladder, I think, attached to a balloon,—or a portable ivory tower or a new plush womb to escape back into."[24] Although there was the usual lightheartedness to his descriptions, the endeavour was deadly serious. Thomas explored every plausible route to avoid military employment to its final inch, before his own ill health brought him the relief he so keenly desired. He did this partly out of fear of personal loss, of course. He

was genuinely terrified by the idea of joining the forces even in a supporting role. But it was also because he could make no sense of his
fundamental commitments—to beauty, to the ordinary, to sentimental attachments to one's fellow beings—at a time of war. Escape
seemed the only option.

This compulsion to find release from the conflict was in no way
reserved to Thomas, of course. There was a spirit of escape in Spender
and Connolly's *Horizon* too. They packed its pages with romantic tales
of happier times, adventures from what they saw as more straightforward conflicts of the past, like the Spanish Civil War, and new poetry that described how one might continue to live as if there were
no war in the present.

One new voice commissioned to write in just this vein was Laurie
Lee. Then a young but already well-travelled man, Lee longed for the
simplicity of romantic adventures in Slad, rural Gloucestershire, the
adventures that would later provide the foundations for his masterpiece, *Cider with Rosie*. Now, his "Invasion Summer," published in *Horizon*'s sixth edition, instantly became a classic of this escapist genre.
The poem was strikingly reminiscent of Thomas Hardy's insistence
during the previous war that love and life in the English countryside
would always prevail against the traumas of conflict. This time,
though, it was tinged with a little more guilt:

> not a word of war as we lie,
> our mouths in a hot nest
> and the flowers advancing.
>
> Does a hill defend itself
> does a river run to earth
> to hide its quaint neutrality?
>
> A boy is shot with England in his brain
> but she lies brazen yet beneath the sun
> she has no honour and she has no fear.[25]

Sincere though Lee was about the advantages of being lost in the country with a lover rather than fighting in France or hiding from the bombs in London, his words betrayed a distinct unease. Carrying on as if nothing had changed by isolating oneself as far as was humanly possible was not a noble strategy. Thomas's argument in the 1930s had been that everyday life mattered more than the grand or the pompous, not because it was an escape from the fundamentals of community life but because only it could provide the real source of what we might call togetherness. Hiding away could not do that. It was too individualistic, too contemptuous of the lives of others who remained exposed. The task remained, then, to find a way of rekindling the spirit of community from the shared experiences of everyday life, even as those experiences were ripped apart.

The unlikely first source of inspiration here was Orwell. In the late 1930s, Orwell had been horrified by the idea of the war more intensely than most of his peers. Well into 1939, his was a rare voice on the left urging against military confrontation with Fascism. But he also more swiftly adjusted himself to the reality of war that anyone else. The reasons for this shift were no doubt complex, but prominent among them was a sense that the war was as likely to be a force for good at home as a force for bad. Far from rendering people more diverse and discordant, that is, Orwell quickly came to the view that it might enable the British people to identify more clearly what it was that they really valued in their common lives and to cleave to it more passionately and with a greater sense of solidarity than they had done during the Depression. People might also be able to name those who stood against them, he thought, not just abroad but at home as well. People who had previously shied away from radical politics, for example, might finally be tempted to call time on the profiteers, the exploitive bosses, and the politicians who were interested only in feathering their own nests and not in serving the common good.

His classic statement of this position appeared in his short book *The Lion and the Unicorn*, written in the last few months of 1940 and published in February 1941. "Are we not forty-six million individuals, all different?" he asked, as if channelling the conclusion of *Between the Acts*. No, he answered, or at least that's not all we are. Instead, there "is something distinctive and recognizable in English civilization" that binds us together. And for Orwell that lay, of course, in the ordinary and the everyday:

> It is somehow bound up with solid breakfasts and gloomy Sundays, smoky towns and winding roads, green fields and red pillarboxes. It has a flavor of its own. Moreover, it is continuous, it stretches into the future and the past, there is something in it that persists, as in a living creature. . . . And above all, it is *your* civilization. It is *you*. However much you hate it or laugh at it, you will never be happy away from it for any length of time. The suet puddings and the red pillarboxes have entered your soul.[26]

The remainder of *The Lion and the Unicorn* was a treatise on the importance of patriotism and economic transformation and an attack on internationalism and capitalism. We shall return to those themes in more detail in the following chapters. But these opening reflections gave a clear indication of just how far Orwell had travelled in the first two years of the war. The everyday habits, practices, and beliefs of the British people were no longer threatened by the war. Rather, they gave the country its only chance to prevail in it. "In war it is civilian morale, especially working-class morale, that is decisive in the long run," Orwell argued, and this morale could only be maintained by celebrating the ties that bind us together, even those that initially appeared insignificant, parochial, and mundane. He was, moreover, distraught that there was "little or no sign that the Government recognizes this."[27] The intellectual battles of the 1930s—between the elitism of both Right and Left, on the one hand, and a faith in ordinary people, on the other—began to play themselves out again, but this time as military strategy. What Britain did not need, Orwell implicitly insisted, was a dictatorial figure on top, along the lines of

The Broad Walk, Regent's Park, 1938
Laing Art Gallery, Newcastle-upon-Tyne, United Kingdom © Tyne & Wear Archives &
Museums/Bridgeman Images

Woolf's Miss La Trobe. It needed instead to release the collective energies of a people already held together by the common culture exhibited in everyday life.

So convinced was Orwell of the power of this new argument that
he wrote to *Time and Tide* in June 1940 to insist that any war effort
grounded in the armed forces alone would inevitable fail. Only so-
called civilians—everyday people—could truly protect the country.
"Our slogan," he explained, "should be ARM THE PEOPLE." "I submit
that the campaign in France and the recent civil war in Spain have
made two facts clear," he continued. "One is that when the civil population is unarmed, parachutists, motor cyclists and stray tanks can
not only work fearful havoc but draw off large bodies of regular troops

who should be opposing the main enemy. The other fact . . . is that the advantages of arming the population outweigh the danger of putting weapons in the wrong hands."[28] Hand grenades and shotguns, he concluded, should be widely distributed as swiftly as possible, and the British should prepare to fight a relentless guerrilla war.[29]

As a potential Nazi invasion loomed, others too were drawn to this emerging idea of a "people's war" as opposed to a war of elites and armies. Chief among them, at least in terms of popular appeal, was Priestley. In 1940, his Sunday-evening radio broadcasts, the *Postscripts*, made him the nation's most recognizable voice after Winston Churchill. And it is not hard to see why. Even when read with the jaundiced eyes of our own century, there is something indisputably magnificent about the *Postscripts*, these short talks for the radio that were never intended to be published, let alone read for decades after.

Priestley regularly began his *Postscripts* with an acknowledgement of the desire to escape, that sense that the important aspects of life— love, beauty, community, and fellow felling—were more easily found away from the conflict than within it. He spoke of the beauty of spring in the English countryside, about "the hay and the barley, about beef and milk and cheese and tobacco," about children playing with their boats on a park pond, and about the escapades of ducks and their ducklings.[30] All of these "triumphant little parcels of life," he reminded his listeners, allow them, even if only momentarily, to forget the war, "the imminence of invasion, the doubts about the French Fleet, the melancholy antics of the Bordeaux Government."[31]

But weekly he would then turn from these observations to the new thought that it was the very same spirit that comforted people, that gave them their sense of belonging, away from the war that would enable them to succeed in it. All of these experiences, after all, provided just that "powerful and rewarding sense of community" that was so desperately required.[32] "We see now," he reported as Britain was bombarded in the Blitz, "it's our nerve *versus* his; that we're not really civilians any longer but a mixed lot of soldiers—machine-minding soldiers, milkmen and postmen soldiers, housewife and mother soldiers—and what a gallant corps that is—even broadcasting soldiers."[33] "This then," he declared in one of his most confident of all the *Postscripts*, "is a wonderful moment for us who are here in London, now the roaring centre of the battlefield, the strangest army the world has ever seen, an army in drab civilian clothes, doing quite ordinary things, an army of all shapes and sizes and ages of folk, but nevertheless a real army, upon whose continuing high and defiant spirit the world's future depends."[34]

The primary challenge, then, was to maintain this "high and defiant spirit." The *Postscripts* crackled with ideas in this regard, some of them more plausible than others and none quite as forceful as Orwell's notion of handing out hand grenades and shotguns. "I'd stop making everything dreary and try and create as much fun, colour, romance as possible," Priestley suggested, introducing a theme to which he would return again and again for the rest of his life. "I'd have bands playing everywhere, and flags flying, and as much swagger and glamour as the moment will stand."[35] He also wanted a big, bold sense of the potential of the future; a sense that this wartime generation of heroes would not be forgotten as the last had been. People should all talk constantly, he insisted, about "what we're all struggling and battling for. Not for some re-grouping on the chess-board of money and power politics; but for new and better homes—real homes—a decent chance at last—new life."[36] "We're not fighting to restore the past; it was the past that brought us to this heavy hour," he would frequently conclude, but "we are fighting to rid ourselves and the world of the evil encumbrance of these Nazis so that we can plan and create a noble future."[37]

For all the rousing talk of the future, however, Priestley, like Orwell, believed that the defiant spirit of the British people was most thoroughly nourished not by utopian dreaming but by the shared experiences of ordinary, everyday life and, during war, that meant it was nourished by the era that had just passed, just as much as, if not more than, it was by any dreams about the future.

Nowhere was this clearer than in the story of the British Expeditionary Force's escape from the beaches of Dunkirk in June 1940, which Priestley, along with Churchill, helped turn into a story of lasting national significance. Dunkirk was the subject of Priestley's very first *Postscript*, and he lost no time establishing the essence of his argument. "Nothing, I feel, could be more English than this Battle of Dunkirk," he began. It was English in its "folly and its grandeur," with poor planning from an out-of-touch military establishment placing the troops' lives in peril just as they were said to have done in the First World War. But it was "also very English (and when I say 'English' I really mean British) in the way in which, when apparently all was lost, so much was gloriously retrieved."[38] And to Priestley's mind what was most characteristically English about it, "so typical of us, so absurd and yet so grand and gallant that you hardly know whether to laugh or to cry," was the part played in evacuation from the beaches "not by the warships, magnificent though they were—but by the little pleasure-steamers."[39]

And there it began. The invocation of ordinary, everyday, unremarkable life, as we used to know it, not only holding us together in sentimental allegiance but actually, practically coming to the nation's rescue at this its most dangerous hour. It is worth quoting a key passage at length:

> We've known them, these fussy little steamers, all our lives. We have watched them load and unload their crowds of holiday passengers—the gents full of high spirits and bottled beer, the ladies eating pork pies, the children sticky with peppermint rock. Sometimes they only went as far as the next seaside resort. But the boldest of them might manage a Channel crossing, to let everybody have a glimpse of Boulogne. . . . Even if they were new, there was always something old-fashioned, a Dickens touch, a mid-Victorian air, about them. They seemed to belong to the same ridiculous holiday world as pierrots and piers, sand castles,

ham-and-egg teas, palmists, automatic machines, and crowded sweating promenades.[40]

Priestley bundled so much into this invocation. A whole way of life, a relationship to place, a childish infectiousness, continuity across time, the coming together of families in public, food and fun; they all enabled the development of the spirit he desired, that spirit of community, the belief that we are better when we are together. There was a fixity, a durability, and a commonality, but also a constant sense of not taking things too seriously and never accepting that the nation was someone else's to shape. This was a world in which people's lives were always circumscribed and made safe by tradition and convention, but also indisputably made their own, both yesterday and today. With all of this, the fundamental idea of the "people's war" was born, and the memory of the everyday was at its very core.

Dylan Thomas was more reluctant than either Orwell or Priestley to embrace this idea, but when he did, he took it to even greater heights. His initial response to the stoicism and steely determination he was surprised to see displayed by so many of those all around him was to find it all rather absurd. "I met a man yesterday who had worked in a high-explosive factory in the last war," Thomas wrote to his friend Clement Davenport in April 1941 when it was still not apparent that he could escape active duty, and that man said, "Oh, don't you worry about it. Everything's all right. I lost the sight of my right eye but I got the O.B.E."[41] As the war progressed, though, Thomas dropped this air of cynical detachment—an air that had never really suited him—and began instead to develop his own distinctive take on the idea that the aspects of ordinary, everyday life that he cherished so much could still play a fundamental role in fostering a sense of togetherness even in the face of the very real evils of war.

That distinctive take began with the poems that would eventually be published as *Deaths and Entrances*, the Second World War's greatest collection of poetry from the home front. Here the fear and melan-

choly that had characterized Thomas's first response to the outbreak
of war met a new, more steely sense of the resilience of ordinary people
trying, sometimes desperately, to go on about their normal lives, even
as others perished around them. The result was some of the most compelling poetry he ever wrote, and none more tellingly combined the
evocation of the everyday and the destructive horrors of the Blitz than
"Among Those Killed in the Dawn Raid Was a Man Aged a Hundred," written for *Life and Letters Today,* in the middle of 1941:

> When the morning was waking over the war
> He put on his clothes and stepped out and he died,
> The locks yawned loose and a blast blew them wide,
> He dropped where he loved on the burst pavement stone
> And the funeral grains of the slaughtered floor.
> . . .
> Dig no more for the chains of his grey-haired heart.
> The heavenly ambulance drawn by a wound
> Assembling waits for the spade's ring on the cage.
> O keep his bones away from that common cart,
> The morning is flying on the wings of his age
> And a hundred storks perch on the sun's right hand.[42]

For all of the resilience they displayed, the poems of *Deaths and
Entrances* were of course still some way from the rhetorical optimism
of Priestley's *Postscripts* and the proud patriotism of Orwell's *Lion and
the Unicorn*. With these poems, Thomas had come out of hiding but
he had yet to lay out his own account of how the spirit of togetherness for which he always aspired could be kept alive during war.

He discovered the answer to that quest in an unlikely place. Having
somewhat ironically begun writing scripts for wartime propaganda
films for a small, independent filmmaker—it was the only reliable
source of paid employment that he could find at the time—Thomas
began to reflect more deeply on the potential sources of morale. He
suddenly needed to know where the characters in his short films were

Crowded Improvised Air Raid Shelter
Bill Brandt © Bill Brandt Archive

going to find their resolve, their determination, and he needed also
to work out what was going to distinguish them from their enemies
in Europe. Little bits of dialogue began to emerge, about both the
future and the past, all of which had the effect of making Thomas
himself believe just a little more in the war effort.

The major breakthrough, though, came right at the beginning of
1943 when the BBC asked him to begin to record a few short talks

for the radio. Although Thomas never came close to rivalling Priestley in broadcast popularity, these talks nonetheless provided him the opportunity to discuss his ideas directly with a large, mainstream audience for the very first time. No one who was familiar with the stories of the 1930s should have been surprised about where his imagination took him as he prepared these broadcasts. It went straight back to childhood, and to the memories of growing up in Swansea, where he made magic out of the raw material of the mundane. He told of messing around in the park, of strolling through the streets of a small seaside village while everyone else slept, and of holidays in August and at Christmas.

On the surface, these reminiscences could appear just another form of escape. They can be read as a return, as it were, to Laurie Lee's trysts in the countryside or Thomas Hardy's sturdy rural workers ignoring the sounds of gunfire in far-off lands. Indeed, many critics have dismissed them as just this over the years. But this is to miss the point. These memories were not a way of avoiding the reality of war. They were a method for dealing with it. They provided, both for Thomas and for all who listened and shared them, what Bonnie Honig calls a "holding environment." The memories, that is, provided the vital psychological sense of something lasting. They were stories that enabled people at risk to feel safe and secure enough to reconnect with themselves and to begin once again to make attachments to each other. In other words, the capacity to conjure and to share these memories of normal life lived before the war—a life lived with laughter, hope, and expectation, and often in harmony with others—provided life with a sense of the very "permanence it lacks."[43] They stabilized the world at the very moment it appeared most fragile.

Thomas did all of this, moreover, in a remarkably everyday fashion. Once again, these were not memories of grand places. They were not celebrations of conventions and traditions laid down by an established elite or by those who thought themselves somehow greater than ordinary. They were memories of experiences that Thomas not only shared with others, but that were *made* by those others too.

This was a point that Thomas learnt to labour for the rest of his career. It would be a major theme in his eventual masterpiece, the 1953 play for voices, *Under Milk Wood*, as we shall see in a later chapter, and often is only associated with that work. But it was strikingly present in these wartime stories, and often delivered with cuttingly caustic humour. "We used to wander past the blackened monuments of civic pride," he recalled, most of all "the museum, which should have been *in* a museum."[44] In their place were riotously affectionate stories of places and events and experiences that had been shaped by just about anyone:

> Never was there such a town (I thought) for the smell of fish and chips on Saturday nights, for the Saturday afternoon cinema matinees where we shouted and hissed our threepences away; for the crowds in the streets, with leeks in their pockets, on International Nights; for the singing that gushed from the smoky doorways of the pubs in the quarters we never should have visited; for the Park, the Park, the inexhaustibly ridiculous and mysterious, the bushy Red-Indian-hiding Park, where the hunchback sat alone.[45]

Thomas knew that there were other risks in investing so much importance in the past. In a concrete sense, the events and experiences he described were already lost by the time he told them. They could not simply be recovered. We do not live in the past. As such, he was aware that some might think of his stories as offering only an illusion of harmony, in the same way Miss La Trobe's pageant presented a fragile and ephemeral story of togetherness in Woolf's *Between the Acts*. Even more than that, he was also aware that his memories were not entirely whole or harmonious themselves. They were always partial. "The recollections of childhood have no order," he told his listeners. They are like "every-coloured and shifting scented shoals that move below the surface of the moment of recollection, one, two, indiscriminately, suddenly, dart out of their revolving waters into the present air: immortal flying fish."[46]

Unlike Woolf, though, Thomas was not led by any of this to believe that the spirit of community that his memories engendered was a fake. Even the very oddly remembered past was, Thomas insisted, no less important than the present or the future. Indeed, if you just allowed them to, these memories could shape every aspect of one's life right here and now. The faces he saw in his childhood days in Swansea, he said, "I can see more clearly . . . than the city-street faces I saw an hour ago." When he recalled the "ugly, lovely" town of Swansea, it once again became present to him, alive, exciting and real. "I do not . . . remember a dream. The reality is there."[47]

Beyond this, the very sense of longing that half-remembered stories unleashed was also a crucial part of the point. The emotions that surge to the surface when one makes a real effort to recall a treasured past and it just slips out of view were at the very crux, Thomas thought, of the spirit of community. The mental effort to re-create a democratic past held people together in the present and allowed them to imagine a future. Those who tried to remember such stories as these would not "disperse" as easily as Woolf imagined, nor would they need some external authority to hold them together. To stay together, people just needed to endeavour to recall the people they had been, the way they had shaped a life together, their chances, dreams. Whatever discord might threaten to engulf the world, "the properties of my memory remain."[48]

Many years later, the American novelist Marilynne Robinson provided a definition of "community" that goes to the very heart of Thomas's wartime broadcasts. Community, she argued, consists in "imaginative love" for people who are not immediately present to us but who we could easily believe are. In other words, it requires us to think about and feel attached to people who are, in fact, elsewhere. We feel *as if* they were sitting immediately next to us, or walking with us on the streets, or drinking with us in the pub, or playing with us in the park. Robinson called this idea "presence in absence."[49] We are held together by our ability to believe that we could share a stable, beautiful, warm world together, either because we once did or because we can easily imagine other people who bear more than a passing resemblance to us once to have done so. This is precisely what Thomas's stories were meant to achieve.

As the war itself edged to a close, this idea of "presence in absence" preoccupied Thomas more than any other. In 1944, a year after he began his BBC broadcasts, he made it the theme of what would become the most celebrated of all of his poems, "Fern Hill." Directly inspired once again by a reading of D. H. Lawrence, "Fern Hill" was published in *Horizon* in the last year of the war.[50] In it, Thomas took the ability of childhood memory to bring reassurance at a time of war, the subject of the broadcasts, and immeasurably deepened it by bringing it face-to-face with the very fact of mortality itself:

> Nothing I care, in the lamb white days, that time would take me
> Up to the swallow thronged loft by the shadow of my hand,
>   In the moon that is always rising,
>   Nor that riding to sleep
>   I should hear him fly with the high fields
> And wake to the farm forever fled from childless land.
> Oh as I was young and easy in the mercy of his means
>   Time held me green and dying
>   Though I sang in my chains like the sea.[51]

Thomas had begun the war blinded and terrified by the threat of war, incapable of writing, of finding a purpose in it, worried that his very life was at an end and that it had all been for nothing. He ended it, a poet and a broadcaster at the height of his powers, capable of dealing even with the inevitability of death itself. A particular kind of everyday memory had released him. With that, the essence of his war-time work was done.

"The past is a curious thing," Orwell reflected in *Coming Up for Air* as the Second World War loomed. "I suppose an hour never passes without you thinking of things that happened ten or twenty years ago," but then sometimes it is far more powerful than that, and "some sight or smell . . . sets you going and the past doesn't merely come back to you, you're actually *in* the past."[52] Orwell could not have known when he wrote these words how powerful they would become. For just a few years later, a certain kind of memory of the past—what we might call a democratic memory, of a rich, everyday culture created by ordinary people themselves—provided the answer to the most pressing of political questions: How were the people of Britain to stay attached to each other, bonded by a spirit of community, at the very time when the nation was thrown into the torment of war?

Crucial though this argument was, however, it could not resolve everything. For all of their power, the memories these writers evoked were predominantly small in their scale and local in their origin. Thomas admitted as much openly in his very first BBC broadcast. Swansea "was my world," he said; "outside, a *strange* Wales." That broader country "moved about its business which was none of mine," and "beyond that unknown Wales lay England which was London."[53] Priestley, too, spoke only of small slices of the country. His tales were of people in seaside towns like Margate, the streets of Blitzed-out London, the rural fields of Yorkshire and the West Country. It was a larger canvass than Thomas's but partial nonetheless. Even Orwell's recollections were circumscribed. For all his talk of a national story, he only ever spoke explicitly about a very distinct part of the nation. His *Lion and the Unicorn* was addressed to the genius of England. It was silent on Wales, Scotland, and Northern Ireland, let alone all the countries beyond, including those still yoked to the United Kingdom by empire.

A further task fell, therefore, to each of these writers and to those who increasingly gathered around them as the war raged. That was the task that our own era's politicians uglily call "scaling up." They not only had to show how these memories of the everyday past could engender a sentiment of collective unity, they had to describe also what these stories of parts of a nation could say about its whole. And they would also have to turn their attention to the ways in which new memories could be shaped, for as the generations passed and the young became old, the memories of the 1920s and 1930s would not do forever. As we will see, words alone would not be enough for this task. Pictures, both moving and still, would also be required. Chapter 4, therefore, begins with the efforts of a man who drew together the sentiments of these stories of community with a set of photographs that sought to evoke the emotions of a whole country, Bill Brandt.

4

All Nations Are Odious, but Some Are Less Odious Than Others

*I*T IS ONE OF the delicious ironies of the British nation that one of the greatest exponents of wartime "Britishness" was not born British himself. Bill Brandt came into the world in Hamburg, Germany, at the outset of the twentieth century and only moved to England in 1931, just as the Depression took hold. He worked steadily through the 1930s, publishing two masterful but largely overlooked collections of photographs, *The English at Home* in 1936 and *A Night in London* in 1938.[1] It was the war that brought him renown. Through pictures of the effects of the conflict on the people and places of Britain—studies of those sheltering from the bombs underground, the abandoned landscapes of industrial Wales, and the threatened wilds of Hadrian's Wall—he became the artist who most effectively displayed the unique and paradoxical experience of the home front. His pictures both caught and helped create a spirit of Britain.

Brandt's images were neither straightforwardly celebratory nor
tragic. They were images of everyday life at war. And as a result, they
were ambivalent. They were hard to read and full of metaphorical
shade, even when high in literal contrast. His photograph of St. Paul's
Cathedral in wartime is a prime example. Brandt's St. Paul's is not
the one that my dad showed me as a child as he told me inspiring
tales at bedtime. That one was taken by Herbert Mason, of Associated Newspapers, and showed St. Paul's towering above the flames,
strong, resilient, capable of inspiring a spirit of optimism even decades
later. Brandt's image was altogether less heroic. In his, the cathedral
is seen only in silhouette, off to the side in the background. The focus
of the picture is on a huge pile of rubble at the front, houses and offices bombed to bits by the night's air attack. St. Paul's still stands. It
offers some hope. But it also appears uncertain, cowed even, worried
about whether it is to face the destructive force next.

This ambivalence was neither accidental nor infrequent for Brandt.
In fact, it was the very core of his vision of the British nation. As the
historian Stephen Brooke has it, there "are sombre undercurrents" in
all of Brandt's photographs that "unsettle" at least as much as they reassure.[2] This spirit of ambivalence separated Brandt from the firebrands
of his age.[3] Nothing in his work suggested propaganda. Even when picturing the despair of working people in the Depression and contrasting
it with the relaxed smugness of the idle rich at play, Brandt steadfastly
refused to politicize his images. As one of his editors recalled, "He had
an acceptance of the world for what it is, and took pleasure in the ap-
parition of its surfaces, and the warm contacts of human beings."[4]

That refusal to politicize his work in any orthodox way has disappointed generations of more ideologically inclined critics ever since.
Some are dismayed that he refused to embrace his new country with
enough flag-waving, patriotic fervor. Others are concerned that he
failed wholeheartedly to demand the abolition of the capitalist system
that so obviously blighted the lives of many of his subjects. But
Brandt's ambivalence was, of course, entirely of a piece with the ideas
that animate this book. None of the writers and artists described here,

St. Paul's Cathedral in the Moonlight, 1942
Bill Brandt © Bill Brandt Archive

after all, were comfortable either with politics as it was standardly practiced or understood, nor were they at ease with traditional ideas of nations and nationhood. There was no room for bombast or idealized abstraction in the worldview that Laurie Lee, George Orwell, J. B. Priestley, and Dylan Thomas spent much of the war shaping in private and advancing in public.

Dylan Thomas, 1941
Bill Brandt © Bill Brandt Archive

In this context it is not surprising that one of Brandt's first wartime works was a portrait for *Picture Post* of Priestley, sunk deep into a garden chair, somehow enjoying a snooze and a pipe simultaneously while on a visit to the English seaside town of Bournemouth. It was joined soon after by portraits for *Lilliput* of Thomas and Lee, among other writers of

J. B. Priestley, 1941
Bill Brandt © Bill Brandt Archive

the time, described as the "new poets of Democracy." Brandt framed
each in their chosen habitats—Thomas in the pub, Lee posed against a
backdrop of classical beauty—but caught them with a quizzical air of
detachment that undercut their youthful energies. With images of this
kind, Brandt revealed that whatever was praiseworthy about Britain

did not come at the expense of ordinariness, uncertainty, or imperfection but instead emerged from those selfsame qualities. The strength of the nation lay not in its vaunted glories but in the varied and unshowy experience of normal life. The implication was that the whole of the war effort depended on what he called an "atmosphere" of Britishness, an atmosphere that helped reveal the country as "familiar yet strange" and managed always to "charge the commonplace with beauty."[5]

But could such a subtle picture of nationhood grounded in the power of everyday life really prevail at a time of such enormous crisis? There could not, after all, have been a more difficult moment to launch an attack on what Orwell dismissively called "all that Rule Britannia" stuff.[6] It was surely reasonable to assume that the very idea of ambivalence would struggle in the inevitably Manichean context of all-out war.

None of the thinkers at the heart of this book were at all comfortable with the idea of nation, for both deeply personal and profoundly intellectual reasons. The root of Brandt's ambivalence is easy to see. Britain offered great hope to Brandt, he revelled in so many of its qualities and charms, but it was never a straightforward place to be. He was an immigrant and suffered so many of both the triumphs and the setbacks that often befall those who tread that path. Before he arrived in London, Brandt had enjoyed the company of the greatest and most celebrated artists of his day in continental Europe. He had studied with Man Ray, counted Georges Braque as a close personal friend, and was courted by those who enjoyed the status of avant-garde. In Britain, he remained almost unknown even eight years after arriving. He lived in a small flat in London's Belsize Park, his route into the artistic establishment blocked and his work sought out only by the often harsh, demanding, and narrowly commercially minded editors of *Picture Post* and *Lilliput* magazines.

Orwell, Priestley, and Thomas had less immediately discernible reasons for their doubts, but those doubts were profound and powerful nonetheless. Each of them had come of intellectual age in the aftermath of the First World War, and they were steeped in the cultural reaction to that conflict. Their instincts were shaped by the dismissals of ideals of England and Englishness, and Britain and Britishness, characterized most by the work of D. H. Lawrence. They had grown up learning to loathe the abstractions that masked the complex and often dark social reality of life in Britain, and there was no abstraction that did that more than the idea of nation and nationhood, especially in the late Victorian and Edwardian form that still predominated in official circles in the early decades of the twentieth century. This was the Englishness espoused by the aristocracy and the fake aristocracy of the upper-middle class. It was a story that hid the realities of social hierarchy and the power of money behind tales of tradition and the practice of pomposity. For the generation that grew up with the horrors of both the trenches and industrial poverty seared into their minds, all this form of nationhood did was obscure the need for change and secure the place of privilege.

Thomas unsurprisingly hated it most of all. Such a way of looking at the world was, he explained, a stunted form of "intellectual and emotional priggery" that he sought always to excise from his work. Artistic expressions of this standard form of British patriotism always read like "a chunk of adulterated Chesterton revised by Sir Edward Elgar," influences that he "hated with all [his] heart."[7] Elgar, the composer of "Land of Hope and Glory," was a frequent point of reference for the young Thomas. He has "inflicted more pedantic wind and blather upon a supine public than any man who has ever lived," Thomas insisted.[8] Nothing seemed further from the everyday realities of life that Thomas adored than traditional British, and actually so often narrowly English, patriotism.

For Orwell, it was the experience of an imperial childhood, an Eton education, and his own service in the police in Burma that directed his ire. What he hated with the intensity that Thomas hated Elgar was the "boasting and flag-waving" of the "swaggering officer type."[9]

Priestley took out his hatred in a way that reflected his own status as a Yorkshireman, someone from outside the conventional mainstream. His disdain was for what he called the "Big Englanders," whom he described as "red-faced, staring, loud-fellows, wanting to go and boss everybody about all over the world, and being surprised and pained and saying, 'Bad show!' if some blighters refused to fag for them." They, he concluded, may be "patriots to a man," but that is precisely why patriotism had such a bad name.[10]

It was not only these negative stereotypes of ruling-class Englishness that drew them away from the idea of nation. As Chapter 3 explained, there was a positive reason to avoid the idea of the nation too. Their enthusiasm for the everyday always took them most directly to the warmth of the parochial. They celebrated the vitality of different parts of the country, those hidden away, never associated with the standard national story. For them, real beauty lay in the family home, in the rundown rural village, and in the suburban streets of the new commuter towns. It was the "clatter of clogs in the Lancashire mill towns, the to-and-fro of the lorries on the Great North Road, the queues outside the Labour Exchanges, the rattle of the pintables in the Soho pubs," that appealed to Orwell. They were what he called the "fragments" of the national scene, so often missing or even incompatible with what went by the name of nationhood.[11]

Even at the very height of the war itself, Thomas wrote in this way. His "Reminiscences of Childhood," broadcast in 1943, longingly recalled a time when he had no interest whatsoever in the nation or nations around him. As a child growing up in the First World War, he recalled, he heard his parents talk of a country "called 'The Front' from which many of our neighbours never came back." It was a blessing of indescribable magnitude that "the only 'front' I knew was the little lobby before our front door." As a child, "I could not understand how so many people never returned from there."[12]

However much they longed for it, the realities of war would not allow this childish innocence to persist, as we saw in Chapter 3. In a conflict that none of them could avoid—however much they wished they could—they simply had to offer some kind of idea of the nation itself. There was, just as Priestley had supposed before the conflict began, "no escape on this planet."[13] But it was more than the fact of state-based violence that redirected them to the need to tell a story of nation. It was the fact of social allegiance itself. For all of their longing to celebrate the local and the particular, that is, none of them could hide from the fact that their reluctance to talk in patriotic terms was an anomaly. They were living among people who were clearly and often instinctively drawn to stories of a national stage. The "vast majority of the people *feel* themselves to be a single nation and are conscious of resembling one another more than they resemble foreigners," Orwell explained in *The Lion and the Unicorn*.[14] "One cannot see the modern world as it is unless one recognizes the overwhelming strength of patriotism, national loyalty." Indeed, all other ideological or spiritual forms were "weak as straw in comparison with it." "Hitler and Mussolini rose to power in their own countries very largely because they could grasp this fact and their opponents could not," Orwell concluded.[15]

As the war progressed, therefore, the struggle that confronted each of them was to provide an account of the value and meaning of nationhood that did not do irreparable damage to the fundamentals of their beliefs. Fortunately, their personal experiences in the war, the broader public experience of the home front itself, and the direction in which the official government's propaganda efforts eventually headed enabled just such a story to emerge.

Brandt, Lee, Orwell, Priestley, and Thomas each found themselves in some parts of the British propaganda machine, making films and broadcasts where they were encouraged to employ their unique feel for everyday people and ordinary ways of life in defence of Britain itself. None of them were initially particularly enthusiastic about the task. Thomas and Orwell worried that it was mere "hack" work lacking both artistic integrity and real intellectual freedom. Lee just thought it was all rather ridiculous. Priestley doubted that he would be allowed the political freedom that he desired, resigning from the BBC after criticism of the first few *Postscript* broadcasts. Eventually, however, each made the genre of wartime propaganda their own, transforming the formulaic scripts of Westminster bureaucrats into films, radio broadcasts, and newspaper stories that poignantly reflected the hopes and dreams of millions of people.

The work they produced in these roles had to leave behind the mournful commitment to everyday memory and the past that had done so much to construct their wartime image of community. It also had to break from their instinctive parochialism. What the authorities wanted, after all, were products that reflected the hopes and aspirations of the people of the country as a whole, not just individual parts of it, and could provide uplift at moments of strain. For their new bosses, the task was to provide accounts of the glory of Britain to call their countrymen to arms. As such, they each had constantly to weave their usual celebrations of individuality and eccentricity into a story for as broad as possible a public. They had, in other words, to give their instinctively local vision a national substance.

Brandt's wartime photography marked the high point of this effort. In 1940, the Ministry of Information commissioned Brandt to record life in London's air-raid shelters as part of its vast project to record life in Britain in wartime for future generations. The results were stunning, bracing even today. These were not the clichés of people sitting around upright pianos in Underground stations. There was no cornily communitarian sense of inevitable national unity; no cheery cockneys singing "Knees Up Mother Brown" or grinning George Formby types strumming their ukuleles. Instead, Brandt caught people fearful and suffering. His Londoners were uncertain that they or their loved ones would see the dawn. And yet somehow at the same time he provoked a sense of national purpose, a feeling of shared commitment, and a fundamental refusal to lose that which was valued most.

Brandt's method to achieve this was unique. Whereas newspaper photographers tended to arrive in the shelters early in the evening, to take photos of people awake and keeping their spirits high, Brandt waited until the small hours so that he could catch people sleeping, piled on top of each other, blankets strewn. In some images, we see men fully clothed to maintain their modesty, apart from their feet, which are bared to keep them cool in the sweltering shelters. In others, there are babies wrapped in home-knitted woollen cardigans slipped into makeshift wooden cupboards for extra safety, their elderly relatives peering concerned at them as they are secured into place. He also caught an occasional sense of the suggestive sexuality that could not have been uncommon in these situations. In one image, a lone young woman stares directly into the lens, the word LADIES spelt out above her on a public convenience as if in an erotic theatre, her eyes wondering what kind of night might unfold in this most exposed of places.

Stephen Brooke describes Brandt's process in this work as an artistic effort to show how "the private [can be] intersected with the public, the individual with the community, not only in the survival of the nation, but in its rebirth."[16] And he is basically right. But the categories were never as clear-cut as that academic summary supposes, nor were the efforts as straightforward. Brandt's images show us an extremely difficult balancing act, both on his own part and on the part of his subjects. Most of all, he shows the enormous efforts people went to in order to maintain, treasure even, aspects of their individual, everyday lives in the heightened and perilous atmosphere of the Blitz. The sensation Brandt was strongest at evoking was respect, not for the kinds of qualities that usually garner respect but for the depth of people's commitment to the fundamental elements of the everyday. Looking at the faces in these photographs even now, it is entirely plausible to believe that the war was won by the resilience of the ever-so-ordinary people of Britain. More than that, it is also possible to appreciate an account where these people were understood to be the foundations of the country itself.

These selfsame sensations were evoked in Dylan Thomas's wartime films. Script-writing for wartime propaganda was never wholly pleasurable for Thomas. In fact, he complained about it bitterly to friends, and his wife, Caitlin, was convinced it detracted from the creative energy that should have been directed to his poetry and she constantly reminded him of that fact. There were, indeed, some topics that Thomas was forced to write about for these movies for which even he could create no spirit. The development of new pharmaceuticals in *Conquest of a Germ* proved a topic with which Thomas could do nothing of interest. Most of the time, however, he managed to invest his scripts with the same combination of the magic and the mundane that he had always sought. Whereas most wartime propaganda films inhabited a world of cliché, grandiosity, or technocracy, Thomas's films had coal miners grumbling about the quality of their housing, soldiers and their wives dreaming of the little details in the new homes they had been promised in the bombed-out cities, and the intense emotional struggles of families both when men headed off to fight and when they came home again and the "old days" did not return as easily as everyone hoped.[17]

As Thomas laboured on these scripts, not only did he transform the nature of the films, the films transformed his own thought in turn. For the first time in his life, after all, Thomas had to find a way to write explicitly about nation and nationhood. He could not avoid it. But he wanted desperately to do it in a way that did not abandon his dedication to the extraordinary power of the everyday. The film in which he did that most successfully was the breathtakingly poetic *Our Country*. Originally conceived as a way of persuading Britain's allies overseas that it was a country worth fighting for, *Our Country* became the most experimental and ambitious of all the films Thomas made for propaganda purposes—perhaps the most demanding made by anyone in Britain in the Second World War. In it, Thomas strove to depict the whole of the nation, revealing what he took to be its fundamental character and laying out the reasons why even those most sceptical of the very idea of nation should believe in it.

Here, the camera flies all across the country, opening in Glasgow and journeying to London, to the white cliffs of Dover, to the orchards and farms of East Anglia, to the markets of the marches, and to the industrial heartlands of South Wales before returning to Scotland and ending with the "faces of fishermen" in Aberdeen. Elements of the brutality of war that so marked Thomas's war poetry, such as captured in *Deaths and Entrances*, survived in the script despite the anxieties of his superiors. A young woman is shown walking home from work imagining what would happen if the bombs began to drop, with "suddenly all the houses falling down on you and everybody you knew lying all dead in the street."[18] As with Brandt before him, Thomas did not hide from the brutalities even when he was under orders to uplift.

Thomas could not resist his trademark localism in *Our Country* either. "Take any direction any road up or down," he had his narrator inform the viewers, and "the island alters round every village corner." But for once the overall image was of a country that had learnt how to come together despite its remaining differences. Most importantly, Thomas wanted to show that Britain was a country where people had learnt to struggle collectively not because of any grand ideals or any faith in the established order but because they had realized they share a deep and abiding love of the elements of life that many had previously dismissed as utterly mundane but which are now at grave risk. There is apple picking and hop picking in the fields in *Our Country*, there are commuters rushing across the platforms at Waterloo Station, there are people listening to music in their kitchens, people haggling and drinking in the pubs, people sitting in contemplative silence on the bus. There is nothing grand. No invocations of past military glories or vast noble ideals. That is, nothing grand apart, once again, for the dome of St. Paul's, briefly shown towering above it all.

There at the top of the dome, Thomas told us, it was possible for one's eyes to "move over London." There, everything and everyone can find "peace under one roof."[19]

This image of a nation built out of ordinary people's everyday struggles, passions, and experiences was the major gift that Brandt, Thomas, and their colleagues provided Britain in the Second World War. We easily forget what a monumental achievement it was because we neglect to notice how far an intellectual distance these artists and writers had travelled since the 1920s and 1930s. In those earlier decades, no one would have believed that a story of nation of this kind was possible. When Thomas was coming of age, Lawrence had condemned all talk of patriotism, T. S. Eliot had dissolved into despair, F. R. Leavis had sought solace in the imagined organic communities of the past, and W. H. Auden and Stephen Spender had condemned the whole social order as grounded on greed. None had conceived of the country as fundamentally built from the experiences of its people, good and bad alike.

Despite all of this, this achievement is far more often mocked than it is celebrated by professional historians who study the Second World War today. Busting the so-called myths of the Blitz has been a mainstay of academic British history for decades now. Ever since the publication of Angus Calder's magisterial *People's War*, it has been a commonplace in academia to condemn all the efforts of national reimagining that took place during the war, bundling everything from Gracie Fields to George Orwell into one.[20] Widely admired works like Sonya Rose's *Which People's War?* thus tell us that "the pull to unity" was "haunted by the spectre of division and difference."[21] What was on offer in the wartime propaganda films, in literature, philosophy, and political treaties, the argument goes, was a dangerous story of false homogeneity, blind to the huge variation in social experience that was actually determined by class, gender, and race. At its worst, all these wartime stories of nationhood are dismissed as fundamentally "exclusionary" stories, as malicious as the worst of nationalist propaganda or the forebear of a modern populism, with a mythical single construct of the authentic "will of the people."

There is undeniable truth in many aspects of this critique. For all of their commitments to the experiences of the everyday, some kinds of people were more present than others in Brandt's photos and Thomas's films. There was almost no explicit reference to homosexuality, depressingly little examination of the inequalities of gender, and no discourse on the different experiences of people of colour.[22] Nonetheless, it seriously misses the mark to dismiss the entire intellectual effort as simplistic communitarianism or a belief in a preexisting, unified, settled "will of the people." Although there were worrying omissions in their work, it was a bold effort to do something new. Despite all of the pressures heaped on them by the Ministry of Information or by their editors and superiors, they never took the easy route and endorsed traditional accounts of the nation, with all their consequent legitimation of conventional class hierarchies and undeserved privileges. Instead, they were constantly searching for ways fundamentally to supersede them. Nor were any of these writers or artists ever to be found celebrating the way the country actually *was* in any straightforward sense. Instead, they were intent on providing an account of what they took to be the best of it, so those elements could be cherished and protected, and a better future emerge for all.

This is revealed with striking clarity when we take the time to examine the core conceptual aspects of the idea of nationhood that Brandt, Orwell, Priestley, Thomas, and others developed during the war. At the risk of artificially formalizing their creative work and turning it into amateur political philosophy, there were four key elements to the story of the everyday nation that they advanced, and it is worth spelling out each in turn.

The first element was their unshakeable commitment to what can be called *smallness*. Even as they were pressed to tell a story of the whole country, they remained passionately committed to the local.

"I wished I had been born early enough to have been called a Little Englander," Priestley wrote in *English Journey* back in the 1930s, and it was an idea that prevailed throughout the war. "That *little* sounds the right note of affection. It is little England I love."[23] In part, this dedication to smallness manifested itself in a loud rejection of the pomposity of the patriotism of the past or of the elite and a conviction that the kind of nationhood that mattered to ordinary people had nothing to do with "Rule Britannia" or "Land of Hope and Glory." "The patriotism of the common people is not vocal or conscious," Orwell wrote in *The Lion and the Unicorn.* "There is no popular poem about Trafalgar or Waterloo"; in fact the only battles that are seared into the memory of the British people are "Mons, Ypres, Gallipoli and Passchendaele, every time a disaster."[24]

This commitment to smallness was also displayed in a brilliant ability to undercut symbols of grandeur and replace them with the images of the everyday. As Orwell had it, all the culture in Britain "that is most truly native centres round things which even when they are communal are not official—the pub, the football match, the back garden, the fireside, and the 'nice cup of tea.'"[25] Again, Brandt's work captured this spirit most crisply of all. His work was all about putting misplaced claims to greatness in their place while simultaneously rendering the ordinary beautiful and extraordinary.

Brandt was already well practiced in this before the war. In 1938, he presented a series of images for *Picture Post* called "A Barmaid's Day." Here, he captured a middle-aged woman who worked in a pub, putting on her makeup, chatting to customers, pouring drinks, and also, most importantly, sitting in a deckchair on a rooftop reading a book, the turrets of the Tower of London and Tower Bridge visible in the distance, clad in a characteristically London grey sky. The fundamentals of the message were there for all to see: people like this are what really makes Britain, Britain, not the historic and architectural symbols to which we usually turn.

Brandt repeated the essence of this effort in the war itself and, remarkably given the context, took it to a new level of irreverence. In one particularly bold shoot, "A Day on the River," he emulated Georges Seurat's *Bathers at Asnières*. Like Seurat, Brandt showed workers relaxing on a hot day by the waterside, but whereas Seurat juxtaposed people at leisure with the chimneys of distant factories, Brandt had the round tower of Windsor Castle clearly visible in the background. He also rendered the people in and around the water far more raucously than Seurat had dared. There are women with cigarettes in hands, children screaming, people who seem to be preparing illicit liaisons, and at least one person with a handkerchief folded on a head to keep off the sun. Here were the ordinary people of Britain displayed as in a saucy seaside postcard, partying under the shadow of the home of the King. The viewer is left in no doubt where Brandt thinks the spirit of the country really lies.

The cheekiness of "A Day on the River" leads directly to the second element of this new vision of the nation: its focus on *individuality and eccentricity*. Britain at its best, the argument went, was not a nation that imposed a clear or formal order on people. It was a nation that recognized that people were different one from another, enjoyed their privacy and their uniqueness, and consequently expected the right either to be left alone or to display their uniqueness in public, as was their wish. As Thomas had it in *Our Country*, even during war, in Britain "each man is alone forever in the midst of the masses of men."[26]

Orwell's rendering of this theme was one of the most important parts of *The Lion and the Unicorn*. England, he famously wrote, is "a nation of stamp-collectors, pigeon-fanciers, amateur carpenters, coupon-snippers, darts-players, crossword-puzzle fans," and this "addiction to hobbies and spare-time occupation" displays the essential "privateness of English life." There is nothing particularly glorious about any of these pastimes, beyond the fact that they are the chosen amusements of distinct individuals unused to being told what to do and preferring to spend their spare time on amusements that for some unknown reason tickle them, whatever those in positions of authority think of them. This was, for Orwell, a core feature of the English nation itself, turned from something mundane into the very essence of "liberty," the idea that each of his fellow citizens deserved "a home of your own, to do what you like in your spare time, to choose your own amusements instead of having them chosen for you from above."[27]

This idea was central for Priestley too. In his most expressly political of texts, *Out of the People,* he called it "originality, enterprise, variety, and flexibility" and placed it directly at odds with the habits of nations where individuals were more driven by the diktats of the state.[28] For that reason, of course, it was further taken to be a constant point of difference with Fascism and, even while the country was formally allied with the Soviet Union, with Communism too. "The power-worship which is the new religion of Europe, and which has infected the English intelligentsia has never touched the common people," Orwell had said with a characteristic sideswipe against Spender, Auden, and colleagues.[29]

Priestley's *Postscripts* also made this a major theme. "Yesterday morning I saw the Nazi film, 'Baptism of Fire,'" Priestley told only his second Sunday-night *Postscript* audience. "This Nazi picture is all 'drums and trombones'—gloom and threats. . . . It's all machines and robot stuff."[30] In contrast, the British always expressed a willingness to stand out against the crowd, like "Two-Tonne Annie," the "very large, elderly woman" from the Isle of Wight, to whose story Priestley often returned. Annie lived her life in "a cheerful tumult," roaring her disdain at "wooly, pussy-footed officialdom," even as they tried to evict her from her house for her own well-being, demonstrating for all to see that the British maintained the "imaginative and romantic" spirit that always kept the bureaucrats and the agents of oppression at bay.[31]

Despite this relentless emphasis on difference and rebellious individuality, the third element of nationhood that each of our writers and artists emphasized was a sense of *rootedness*. At the very same time that the French philosopher-in-exile Simone Weil was poignantly writing that "to be rooted is perhaps the most important and least recognized need of the human soul," so the same argument came from those who feared that the deep attachments to place and to a particular people were about to be ripped apart forever.[32] As Thomas put it, despite all of his experimentalism and all of his commitment to the distinctiveness of each and every one of us, ultimately "we're all traditionalists." Or rather, "we're bound to be traditionalists if we're going to be any good at all."[33]

As ever, this commitment to rootedness began with a celebration of the local. "Perhaps the only solidly real place we ever know is the place in which we spent our childhood and youth," Priestley opened one of his last *Postscripts* by saying, and that spirit was widely shared. But as we have seen, the pressures of the war largely morphed this into a claim about nationhood itself. "What can the England of 1940 have in common with the England of 1840?" Orwell asked. The same, he said, as you have in common "with the child of five whose photograph your mother keeps on the mantelpiece." In other words, nothing "except that you happen to be the same person."[34]

Of course, for Orwell and his contemporaries it was a particular kind of repetition through the ages that enabled this sense of rootedness and continuity to prevail: the everyday patterns of everyday life. Once again, Brandt captured the idea perfectly. His masterful collection *A Night in London* showed the city from the time the sun goes down to the time it rises, with the implication that this is a pattern night after night, week after week, month after month. As his biographer Paul Delany explains, the point was inherently conservative: "Every night, events repeat themselves to give the city its familiar character—pleasure-seekers go to the theatre, the policeman pounds his beat, fish arrives at the market, and so on to infinity."[35]

Five years later, Thomas borrowed the same device for *Our Country*, with the repeated rhythms of a single day—a single *every* day— providing reassurance to people faced with the horror of destruction and death. In case it was missed, Thomas's script spelt it out with a rare explicit statement of purpose: "All the separate movements of the morning crowds are lost together in the heartbeat of clocks."[36] He would return to the same idea a few years after the war in *Under Milk Wood*, where the continual, rhythmic beating of the "slow black, crow black, fishing-boat bobbing" sea underscores the rhythmic patterns of a single day as it moves from the dream-filled hush of the night through the raucous hopes and fears of the morning and afternoon back into dream-filled night again: "Listen, it is night moving in the streets. . . . It is the grass growing on Llareggub hill."[37]

If this commitment to roots and to rhythms was the most conservative element of the story of nation, the fourth element was its most radical. This was an insistence on the need, despite it all, for dramatic and far-reaching economic and political *change*. It was a fundamental fact about Britain in all of its constituent parts, they agreed, that it was characterized by social injustice that had to be put right. Put bluntly, the wrong people were in charge and the wrong people were benefitting from what little prosperity there was. To be the nation it really has the potential to be, Orwell insisted, "England has got to assume its real shape." For the nation truly to be of value, the "England that is only just beneath the surface, in the factories and the newspaper offices, in the aeroplanes and the submarines, has got to take charge of its own destiny."[38]

This theme was pursued relentlessly, with no apology. "Right through our national life we have got to fight against privilege, against the notion that a half-witted public schoolboy is better for command than an intelligent mechanic," Orwell stressed near the outset of *The Lion and the Unicorn*. Later, the language was more colourful still: "The heirs of Nelson and Cromwell are not in the House of Lords. They are in the fields and the streets, in the factories and the armed forces, in the four-ale bar and the suburban back garden; and at present they are still kept under by a generation of ghosts."[39] Thomas made the argument even in the midst of his propaganda films, often with the kind of flourish Bertolt Brecht would have appreciated. In *These Are the Men*, he told of the people who really mattered, and the people whose voices have not been heeded enough in the past:

> We are the makers the workers the farmers the sailors
> The tailors the carpenters the colliers the fishermen,
> *We* dig the soil and the rock, *we* plough the land and the sea,
> So that all men may eat and be warm under the common sun.[40]

In *Unconquerable People*, he continued the theme, describing the real heroes of the war in a way that closed with a not-so-subtle reference to Clause IV of the Constitution of the Labour Party, which promised to secure workers "whether by hand or by brain the full fruit of their labour":

> We were small farmers and country labourers
> timbermen trappers who had never seen the towns
> townsmen mechanics clerks and tradesmen
> drivers of cattle and lorries and cranes
> painters of canvasses painters of houses
> cobblers teachers thinkers men from the dockyards
> and shipyards factories ships and trains
> fishermen poets miners carpenters
> the men who worked with their hands and their brains . . . [41]

What all of this meant was that the vision of nationhood spelt out in the Second World War by Brandt, Orwell, Priestley, and Thomas was both far more subtle and far more critical than the majority of recent historians have noticed. The strengths of the British nation—which was often, but not always, read as the English nation—came from its resistance to grandiosity and pomposity, its celebration of individuality and eccentricity, the rootedness that came from the persistence of its everyday rhythms over time, and from the growing realization that huge change is required, change that would alter the balance of power and the distribution of privilege forever.

There were occasional strayings away from the self-consciously everyday and into hyperbole—as when Priestley spoke of "the Dome and Cross of St. Paul's" as the "enduring symbol of reason and Christian ethics seen against the crimson glare of unreason and savagery."[42] But largely this was a grounded, ambivalent, even paradoxical nationalism. It was an account of the nation that saw both strength and weaknesses, hope and suffering, which celebrated the local at the same time as it acknowledged the pull of the whole, and one that treasured both memories of the past and hopes for the future together. It also acknowledged how much work there was to do, accepting even at time of war that there were deep difficulties that came from the very idea of celebrating nation. "All nations are odious, but some are less odious than others," was how E. M. Forster summarized Orwell's view, even in *The Lion and the Unicorn*.[43] It was a significant intellectual feat.

This is not, however, to denude the critics of accuracy altogether. For there was one glaring omission from this group's thinking about the nation: its relationship with empire and the injustices that attended to race.

Empire hardly got a mention. The United States is widely discussed, and Germany and the Soviet Union are analyzed in Priestley's major wartime political treatise, *Out of the People*, for example, but the British dominions and colonies merit no mention at all. And even when there were explicit discussions of the empire, they were far from engaging. The least imaginative or intelligent film script that Thomas produced during the war was his bizarrely straitlaced *Battle for Freedom*, which was intended to tell the story of Britain's relationship to the other countries of empire. It was worse even that *Conquest of a Germ*.

Here, presumably under strict instructions from his superiors, Thomas celebrated the wartime contribution that he apparently unironically described as the "free men of the Empire." The script displays both a horrific political naivety and an entire lack of the warm, humane descriptions that inflected almost all of his other work. "Out of South Africa," it ran at one point, "from the men of different races, colours, ways of thinking, came the will to fight, under the leadership of Field Marshal Smuts, against the enemies of freedom."[44]

Priestley's and Thomas's absence of concern for empire might have come as little surprise. But the same was not true of Orwell. Before the war, he had a long personal history of writing sensitively and intelligently about the perils of belonging to a country with such a baleful record in subjugating other peoples across the world. Although far from entirely unproblematic, essays such as "Shooting an Elephant," which imaginatively drew on his personal experiences as a subdivisional police officer in Burma, at least revealed a willingness on Orwell's part to acknowledge the bitterness and hatred that inevitably accompanied colonial occupation.[45] This personal conviction continued through the war. He regularly used his "As I Please" column for the left-wing Labour newspaper, *Tribune,* for example, to criticize particular absurdities of British imperialism, especially as they concerned India, with which he was deeply engaged, not least because of his job working on the BBC's India service. Nor did he ever hold back on his generalized disdain for the imperial project. Even as late as 1944, he was still willing sometimes to declare that "there is quite a strong case for saying that British imperialism is actually worse than Nazism," which was quite a statement as British troops were dying from bullets and shells on the beaches of Normandy.[46]

Despite all of this, Orwell remained resolutely unable to bring himself to think aloud about the consequences of the association between such an evil and the fundamental characteristics of the everyday British or English nation itself. Britain might be an imperial power, but the British people were not imperialists. More than that, they were not even significantly shaped by imperialism. Their habits, practices, values, and beliefs owed nothing to the imperial experience. His evidence for this initially unconvincing claim lay, in part, in his suggestion that the major decisions about Britain's world status continued to be made by a narrow elite and were not yet subject to serious democratic scrutiny. But it also lay in his sociological observation that the realities of empire rarely intruded into the British everyday. The values and practices of England, that is, went on as if the empire were not there. The worst that could be said of this, Orwell concluded, was that this was a form of collective denial. "It is quite true that the English are hypocritical about their Empire," he said in *The Lion and the Unicorn*. "In the working class this hypocrisy takes the form of not knowing that the Empire exists." But there was no more serious blame to take than that.[47]

These failings to think seriously about empire had deep roots. It reflected the discomfort with cosmopolitanism and internationalism that was long a characteristic of their thought. "I shall never be one of those grand cosmopolitan authors who have to do three chapters in a special village in Southern Spain and then the next three in another special place in the neighbourhood in Vienna," Priestley had written in *English Journey*, and it was a sentiment that Thomas shared.[48] Thomas did occasionally reference faraway places in his writings, but he always saw them through the eyes of people "here" rather than "there," as when he imagined "the antipodes that hang their koala-bears and Maoris, and boomerangs, upside down over the backs of the stars."[49] Even Orwell revelled in what he saw as the mild-mannered xenophobia of the English people. The "English working class are outstanding in their abhorrence of foreign habits," he once put it. "Even when they are obliged to live abroad for years, they refuse either to accustom themselves to foreign food or to learn foreign languages. Nearly every Englishman of working-class origin considers it effeminate to pronounce a foreign word correctly."[50]

None of this was meant as criticism; all of it was delivered with a smile. Most worryingly of all, this absence of concern with a scepticism of others occasionally drifted into an actual open hostility to people who moved to Britain from abroad. While other celebrated wartime writers, such as Elizabeth Bowen, warmly embraced the influx of international exiles into London, evocatively capturing the way it ruptured the tired conventions of the English social scene in their work, there was almost nothing of this in the writings of Orwell, Priestley, or Thomas. Quite to the contrary, their writing sometimes gave the distinct impression that they would rather people of different nationalities and different ethnicities be kept apart. It was not just that people originating from different lands were invisible in their work; it often seemed that they had been intentionally hidden. And even worse, when they did come into view, they were sometimes singled out with contempt.

Priestley was the most straightforward in expressing his disdain. *English Journey*, which is so beguiling, kind, and compassionate in many ways, was utterly dismissive of those who had come to Britain from overseas. Of the multicultural communities of the Liverpool docklands, he wrote, "Port Said and Bombay, Zanzibar and Hongkong [sic] had called here," and as a result there "cannot be a queerer class anywhere in the world. The wooly curls of the Negro, the smooth brown skin of the Malay, the diagonal eye of the Chinese, they were all there, crazily combined with features that had arrived in Lancashire by way of half a dozen different European countries, from Scandinavia to Italy."[51] But even this was as nothing in comparison with his open contempt for immigrants from Ireland, to whom he unapologetically attributed the spread of "ignorance and dirt and drunkenness and disease." The "Irishman in England," he argued, "has lost his peasant virtues, whatever they are, and has acquired no others." On arriving in England, the Irish "have settled in the nearest poor quarter and turned it into a slum, or, finding a slum, have promptly settled down to out-slum it."[52]

Such narrow-minded racism was not new, of course. Both anti-Irish and anti-immigrant sentiment had been a commonplace of political campaigning in Britain ever since the late nineteenth century. A simple tour around any museum exhibit of leaflets and posters from this era's political campaigning gives ample witness to that. It was rarer among, of course, those who associated themselves with the political left than the right, but certainly not unknown to socialists and Communists too. More importantly for our concerns, though, it had also long been associated with poets and writers who celebrated local attachment and place. As the literary critic Fiona Stafford puts it, "The thronging streets, filled with a bewildering mass of . . . immigrants, and foreign visitors," often appeared "completely antithetical" to those who cleaved to an "ideal of hardy individuals rooted in their native soil," and that had been true at least since the eighteenth century.[53]

There is, nonetheless, something profoundly depressing about the inability of Orwell, Priestley, Thomas, or any of the others who shared their general disposition to produce an alternative view in these wartime years. Their thinking was, after all, characterized by an ability to humanize those whom others had rendered inhuman by concentrating on the mundane fundamentals of everyday life; fundamentals like family, friendship, childhood, and romance. There is no reason why these selfsame experiences could not have been generalized in some way beyond borders and beyond a single ethnicity to a broader human group. There is no reason, in other words, why the "imaginative love for people not immediately present to them" that was the core of their practice could not have extended beyond the boundaries of the nation as conventionally conceived. It should have been. And those of us who are otherwise sympathetic to their vision must take note of the fact that it was not and think on how we should respond.

In comparison with my parents and their parents before them, I have been fortunate not (yet at least) to live through a world war. In my lifetime, British international competition has taken a different form. Sometimes that has unmistakable downs, as with the turgid political debates around Brexit and the scramble to respond to COVID-19. At other times, it has created huge highs, as when Britain has presented itself to the world in ways that have lifted the spirit and made the impossible seem briefly possible once again.

One of those times was the London Olympic Games of 2012. Although it may seem like hyperbole to some, Friday, 27 July 2012, genuinely was one of the happiest days of my life. On that night, the games opened in Stratford, in the London borough of Newham. I was living at the time with my wife, Lizzy, in an attic flat in Highbury, North London. From the little window in our kitchen, we could see the top of the newly built Olympic stadium, with its strange little pyramid lights jutting off the roof. We watched the ceremony that night on the television, sending our friends around town text messages to see if they were watching too, and we pushed our heads out of that window now and again to see if we could see the lights and hear the roar of the crowd.

Being a largely melancholic city at the time, no one in London expected very much of the ceremony that night. But everything changed as it got started. With a massive rhythmic beating of drums, an ecstatic volunteer army drawn largely from the communities that lived immediately around the stadium gave instant witness to the fact that this was going to be a ceremony like no other. It was a story of nationhood, from the Industrial Revolution to the austere postindustrial present, told through the lives not of the great and the good but of the everyday people of the country. The heroes of the story were the miners and the factory workers, the nurses of the National Health Service, the teenagers who came of age in the postwar suburbs surrounded by the sounds of music that captivates the world to this day. When the fireworks for the finale went off (which I hopelessly tried to record through the window on my phone for posterity), even the hardest of antipatriotic hearts was softened.

The next day was amazing. Early in the morning, I dropped into the unprepossessing Budgens supermarket just up the road in Islington's Upper Street. It is not the kind of place where people stay long. There is just nothing very pleasant about it. But that morning, people stopped and talked. They looked at the newspaper headlines, all basking in the glory of the night before, and they shared their favourite moments, smiled, teared up, and then laughed at themselves for getting so carried away.

Momentarily, we hoped that was the beginning of something new for Britain. Danny Boyle, the director, and Frank Cottrell-Boyce, the writer, had given us a gift, and we surely wouldn't forget it. But, of course, we did. The warm, inclusive, democratic national story that we all shared that night soon shrivelled. And more than anything, it was politics that did for it. A few of us tried to keep it going. Partly on the advice of Tony Blair, the Labour leader Ed Miliband asked me to write his annual conference speech that year on the idea of everyday nationhood, using Boyle's summary as its jumping-off point. But the era of public spending cutbacks and growing unease about immigration did for it soon enough. Just two years later, the United Kingdom Independence Party came top of the polls in a national election for the first time, and it wasn't long before the country found itself embroiled in Brexit, the most divisive debate since the Second World War.

The vision of nation that Bill Brandt gave us sixty years earlier was, of course, born in much more demanding circumstances than Boyle's, and perhaps that is why it lasted a little longer. But it too began to struggle almost as soon as it emerged. And it was politics that did for that too. In this case, though, it was not the rise of the political right that caused the difficulties. There was no United Kingdom Independence Party in 1945. Instead, it was the triumph of the political left. For although Brandt, Orwell, Priestley, Thomas, Lee, and almost all of their colleagues counted themselves as progressives, leaning distinctly to the left, and probably each voted for the Labour Party in the general election that followed the war in Europe's successful close, none of them could settle with what happened next. In other words, their story of the nation grounded in the power of the everyday was not ready for the socialists in power.

5

The Socialists in Power

WHEN I WAS ABOUT fifteen years old, I read my first explicitly political book. It was a dusty old copy of Clement Attlee's autobiography, *As It Happened,* that my dad had found shoved into a corner of an overcrowded bookcase at home.[1] There probably weren't many teenagers in Britain settling down with Attlee in the late 1980s—in fact, even seasoned scholars find Attlee's prose a bit dull—but I was utterly captivated. Growing up in a South Wales blighted by mass unemployment, I was angry at the Labour Party's continual inability to come even close to beating Margaret Thatcher, and I was desperate to know how it had happened for Attlee. After all, not only had he won an election in 1945, but he had won by an absolute landslide, and not against any old Conservative leader but against Winston Churchill, the man who many would have us believe had single-handedly won the war for Britain. Even more than that, Attlee's government turned out to be not just any other government. It re-constructed fundamental aspects of British life, nationalizing a fifth of British industry, securing full employment, creating a proper social security system for those unable to work, and building the National Health Service. It was fair to say that a few chapters in and Attlee was my hero.

Now, more than thirty years later, the Attlee fan club has grown bigger. Having been told for years that Britain can't afford decent so-cial services or investment in education or to risk taking on the ex-cesses of executive pay, many look back in wonder to a government that did all of those even though the country was almost bankrupted by war. There still might not be many teenagers rifling through the pages of As It Happened, but many thousands of normally unpolitical people have seen Ken Loach's unapologetically hagiographic film, The Spirit of '45, on university campuses and in town halls and commu-nity centres across Britain. Alert to that popularity, it is a rare Labour politician now, young or old, who does not publicly praise the re-forming zeal of Attlee and at least a handful of his cabinet of giants and future giants, Aneurin Bevan, Ernest Bevin, Herbert Morrison, Ellen Wilkinson, and Harold Wilson. Indeed, such praise is not re-stricted to Labour. There's little that unites people in British politics in these polarized times, but the belief that Attlee's government helped Britain off its knees after more than a decade of depression and war is one thing that does.

Much of that enthusiasm was shared at the time. No one wins a landslide election victory without its fair share of excitement. Of course, as anyone who has watched Netflix's The Crown knows, it only took six years for enough dissatisfaction with Attlee's government to grow for Churchill to have his electoral revenge. But in 1945, change was very much in the air, and Labour was its electoral representative. Almost everyone, even conservatively minded writers like T. S. Eliot and F. R. Leavis, agreed that mass unemployment had to be tackled, wealth had to be more fairly distributed, and social services had to be made available to all. The horrors of the Depression could never be repeated; the promise made to this wartime generation had to be fulfilled in a way it had not been to the last.[2]

Despite all of this, the way in which Attlee's Labour government went about its task infuriated many, including those like George Orwell, J. B. Priestley, and Dylan Thomas who clearly identified with the Left. To them, far from following through on the promise of the war, as the government always insisted, it was breaking its word. Britain had just won a "people's war," a war fought around a vision that honoured the ordinary and the everyday, that recognized the distinctive treasures of the parochial and the small, that cherished individuality and eccentricity and was nervous about the big, booming voices of the powerful and the prestigious and was opposed to senseless centralization. But now at the very moment of its triumph, it appeared that all of that might be lost.

Part of this worry centred on the reckless way that Attlee and his colleagues seemed to treat the past. Labour's 1945 election manifesto, *Let Us Face the Future*, was unrelenting in its assertion that Britain was going to be new. Slums were going to be cleared, industries nationalized, and a new welfare state built. In the election campaign, there was talk of a "New Jerusalem" and Labour's posters and pamphlets painted a vision of the future where everything was fresh and shiny and hygienic. For all the passion of the true believers, this relentless modernism generated an unnerving worry for others. What if in the rush to make everything modern and new, crucial elements of the old that really mattered to people were lost? After Attlee's victory, Bill Brandt hurried to photograph parts of the country that he worried were about to be reformed out of existence. "The Vanished Ports of England," "Farewell to London," "The Doomed East End," and "The Forgotten Gorbals"—even the titles of his postwar photoessays reveal his sense of loss.[3] Likewise, Laurie Lee, confronted with a country hurtling towards the future, felt an overwhelming desire to return to the Gloucestershire countryside of his childhood to chronicle his memories as far away from the modernizing enthusiasm of the Attlee years as it was possible to be. The resulting story, *Cider with Rosie*, was everything that the enthusiasts of Attlee's government were not: proud of its parochialism, rooted in the past, comfortable with routine, uncertain about the future.[4]

It was not just the past that was at risk. The perceived recklessness went further than that. In fact, the whole governing project seemed infected with hubris. Attlee's Labour Party seemed to believe that almost anything could be achieved with a bit of expertise, a proper plan, and confident action led from Whitehall and Westminster. This betrayed a belief that experts, officials, and politicians knew what the country really needed and how it should get there, and ordinary people did not. This was never going to be an attractive position for those who had spent at least a decade calling out the errors of elitism. "Politicians and senior civil servants are beginning to decide how the rest of us should live," Priestley complained in an editorial for the mass-market *Sunday Pictorial*.[5] "The rain has stopped, thank Jesus," Thomas wrote just four days after Attlee won; have "the Socialists-in-power-now stopped it?"[6]

There was more than just a negative critique here too. There was a sense of huge missed opportunity. Surely, if a country at war had created a vision of nationhood grounded in the ordinary, then it must be possible to build a politics that did so as well? A politics that was capable of driving the change that was needed at the same time as it preserved that which was worth preserving; a politics that could draw on the expertise needed to change the economic system while simultaneously maintaining faith in the virtue, intelligence, and expectations of ordinary people themselves. "We may expect great achievements from the people," Priestley said, but only if we change the way that politics works. "Politics must no longer be like professional football, in which a few men play while a hundred thousand others look on," he continued. "It must be more like village cricket. Where there are more on the field than round it. If the people make a hash of it, then let them, for at least it will be their own hash."[7]

This became the crucial final challenge confronting those con-structing the public philosophy that lies at the heart of this book. Having carefully shaped ideas of community and nationhood rooted in the extraordinary potential of the everyday, they had now to de-velop a theory of politics that did the same. But precisely what kind of politics would that be? How should the balance between "popular" power and "expert" power rightly be struck? What place should there be for local government as opposed to national? What liberties should remain with the individual at a time of radical reform? What protec-tions, if any, did private industries deserve as the government sought to regulate them or buy them out? How could political parties adapt to make them more open to the influences of the everyday? Did it even make sense to think of politics and the everyday as parts of the same worldview?

Answering these questions turned out to be the hardest challenge of all. In fact, it defeated some entirely, leading them into depths of intellectual and emotional despair that exceeded even those of the opening days of the war. Nonetheless, it was also the challenge from which we stand to learn most today. After all, if politics itself, with all of its hierarchies and hatreds, it scheming and schisms, could be reshaped to accommodate the rhythms of everyday life, then we need to know how in our own times more than almost ever before.

"I do not speak of parliaments and committees," Dylan Thomas wrote to Pamela Hansford Johnson in 1933. They are "eternally ugly things . . . composed of a collection of ugly minds."[8] She did not argue. Disdain for all things conventionally political was widespread among writers and artists throughout the Depression and into the war. Pre-cious little of the partisan political turmoil of the period—the rise of the Labour Party, the collapse of the Liberals, the failures and then resurrection of the Conservatives—attracted any attention from those discussed in this book. Neither did they exhibit any great interest in trends in political philosophy. Whole movements in theorizing rose and fell without them appearing to notice, even movements like the anarchistic and democratically inclined guild socialism with which they might have been expected to share allegiance. The trend, rather, was for fairly broad-brushed critique. Conservative thinkers felt contemporary politics did little to restore the respect for authority the country had lost; radicals argued that it was not up to the task of bringing about the dramatic social and economic change that was needed; romantics felt that the whole thing was just too sordid to be worthy of their time.[9]

As with so many issues, it was D. H. Lawrence who did most to provide real intellectual substance to this generalized dislike. Throughout his essays, short stories, and novels, Lawrence insisted that politics as usually practiced was undone by three fundamental flaws. First, as a vocation it attracted fundamentally undesirable people: egomaniacs wrapped up in their own interests, largely incapable of caring about the interests of others. Second, even when such people could be wrested out of thinking only of themselves, they tended only to think of the most narrowly material concerns, such as the economic interests of the social classes, rather than anything more vital or humane. They had no romance or soul or spirit but dwelled only in thoughts of money and property. "That's politics," Lawrence wrote in his great novel of political despair, *Kangaroo*, "a game for the base people with no human soul left in them."[10] Third, despite, or perhaps because of, these personal limitations, politicians were also always to be found speaking in grand, vaulting abstractions, such as the "Rights of Man, Equality of Man, Social Perfectibility of Man," rather than in the ordinary, concrete prose suited to a description of reality as it actually was. This had the momentary effect of making their ideas sound lofty and admirable, but it also entailed that their words quickly dissolved into meaningless nothingness—what Lawrence called "gewgaw and nonsense"—when studied up close. What most politicians were offering was little more than a simple advertising con trick, Lawrence felt, and he was amazed more people hadn't seen through it. "We have just enough sense not to talk of Ideal

Selfridges or Ideal Krupps or Ideal Heidsiecks," but somehow people still talked of an ideal politics.[11]

This tendency for politicians to hide their basest desires behind grandiose, abstract rhetoric became an increasingly pressing concern as the truth emerged through the 1930s and 1940s about Communism in the Soviet Union. Nothing, after all, better exemplified the horrific consequences that follow dressing up dark realities in idealized abstractions than Stalinist oppression. Revealing this fundamental truth and warning his contemporaries to avoid it at all costs was the essential driver of George Orwell's writing from the mid-1940s until his death in 1951. "My wife and I both saw innocent people being thrown into prison," Orwell recalled from his time in the Spanish Civil War, but "on our return to England we found numerous sensible and well-informed observers" falling for the most "fantastic accounts" of why such imprisonments—and worse—were necessary to protect the gains of the revolution.[12] Persuading as many people as possible to call out these grand lies, or at the very least not to fall for them themselves, was the fundamental mission that lay behind both *Animal Farm*, published just weeks after Attlee's victory, and *Nineteen Eighty-Four*, published three years later. It is the contribution for which history will remember Orwell best.

Orwell was utterly fixated on the evils of political abstraction in these years. "The whole tendency of modern prose is away from concreteness," he insisted in "Politics and the English Language."[13] And this "decay of language" was contributing directly to the "the present political chaos."[14] In one particularly impressive passage, he continued,

In prose, the worst thing you can do with words is to surrender to them. When you think of a concrete object, you think wordlessly, and then, if you want to describe the thing you have been visualizing, you probably hunt around till you find the exact words that seem to fit it. When you think of something abstract

you are more inclined to use words from the start, and unless you
make a conscious effort to prevent it, the existing dialect will
come rushing in and do the job for you, at the expense of blur-
ring or changing your meaning.[15]

Seen this way, the problem of abstraction was that it left issues
vague and uncertain, with people relying on preexisting terminology
to fill gaps in their thinking at the expense of being able to develop
more clear and concrete responses to problems that might actually
help. At other times, though, Orwell argued that the problem of abstraction was almost the opposite: that it permitted an overly certain
politics. If people's political terminology was vague and had only shaky
relationships to concrete realities, that is, then they could get away
without testing their claims and carry on regardless of the facts. They
could continue to believe, or act as if they believed, they were speaking
truth because their assertions were based on no testable claims; they
could reject criticism as failing to see the heart of the matter, because
there was in reality no heart of the matter there.

Orwell was convinced that this abstraction in language gave terrifying cover to the worst of political trends in both capitalist and
Communist society in the 1940s. Since as far back as *The Road to
Wigan Pier*, he had warned that it was becoming "meaningless to
oppose . . . the beehive State, for the beehive State is *here*."[16] But his
anxiety deepened as the years progressed. Politicians everywhere now
seemed intent on oppressing their opponents and regimenting and
regulating everyone else, irrespective of whether they were on the left
or the right. The prevailing "economic system in which land, factories, mines and transport are owned privately and operated solely
for profit—*does not work*," Orwell decisively announced in *The Lion
and the Unicorn*, but his fears about its most obvious alternative—
the *government* control of ownership of industry, which he called
"collectivism"—were equally ferocious.[17] "It cannot be said too often,"
he wrote in the *Observer* in 1944, that collectivism "gives to a tyran-

nical minority such powers as the Spanish Inquisitors never dreamed of." "Capitalism leads to dole queues, the scramble for markets and war," he continued, but "collectivism leads to concentration camps, leader worship, and war."[18]

The use of abstract language was not just at fault because it masked this political reality; it was also at fault because it hindered the development of any plausible alternative. Orwell shaped this argument in a superb, but much overlooked, essay that he published under a different pseudonym in *Tribune* in 1944, called "Can Socialists Be Happy?" Here, he insisted that the fundamental difficulty facing all serious socialist reformers was that they were incapable of describing a better future in anything other than vague and practically impossible abstractions, and as such they had no real idea of the world they were trying to build. This, he insisted, was a direct result of their belief that they had to describe a utopia—a perfect society—before they started acting, when, in fact, they would be much better off thinking and talking about much more discrete realities. Utopias, Orwell argued, are effectively impossible to describe in any compelling detail both because they are future states not grounded in our knowledge of reality and because the human mind cannot meaningfully think as broadly as they require. As a result, people grab hold of some specific fact that they do know and build a vision around that, generalizing from the particular to the universal without acknowledging that is what they are doing. "Nearly all creators of Utopia have resembled the man who has toothache, and therefore thinks happiness consists in not having toothache," he explained. "The wiser course would be to say that there are certain lines along which humanity must move, the grand strategy is mapped out, but detailed prophecy is not our business. Whoever tries to imagine perfection simply reveals his own emptiness."[19]

A further failing of utopias for Orwell was that the elements of human life that go missing from them are precisely the elements that he had learnt to care about most: the ordinary and everyday. The tendency of abstract political thinking, that is, is to focus on the grand and the big, but to forget what makes human life actually worth living. There was no place in any of the utopias known to Orwell for the day-to-day wrangling of life: the arguments of friends and family, the nostalgia for childhood, the pain of lost loves, the sentimental attachment to unremarkable places, the deep if momentary absorption in simple pleasures. Instead, "all efforts to describe permanent happiness have been failures" because they "are invariably unappetizing, and usually lacking in vitality as well." Taking H. G. Wells as an example, Orwell went on: "We all want to abolish the things Wells wants to abolish. But is there anyone who actually wants to live in a Wellsian utopia? On the contrary, not to live in a world like that, not to wake up in a hygienic garden suburb infested by naked schoolmarms, has actually become a conscious political motive." Orwell even detected this fault in his literary hero, Jonathan Swift, whose utopia in *Gulliver's Travels* he found full of "remarkably dreary creatures" who "live uneventful, subdued, 'reasonable' lives, free not only from quarrels, disorder or insecurity of any kind, but also from 'passion,' including physical love." Such characters "choose their mates on eugenic principles, avoid excesses of affection," and, unsurprisingly, "appear somewhat glad to die when their time comes."[20]

Given this failing, Orwell worried that only two fates faced those who were interested in political reform. Either their efforts would be rendered weak and ineffective, as their implausible ideas failed to get real traction in a complex, concrete world, or they would end up like the Soviets, using grand illusions as the cover for the worst kind of oppressive excesses, masking their basest of desires in the garb of political grandiosity, just as Lawrence had warned.

Most of the time, Orwell believed that it was the first of those two fates that was the most likely to befall Britain. His standard worry about Attlee's government, that is, was not that it was about to turn Britain into an oppressive dictatorship but rather that it would end up speaking loudly and bombastically about the promise of a wholly changed society—a "New Jerusalem"—but achieving little because its grandeur detached it from reality. "In the social set-up," he said one year into Attlee's time as prime minister, "there is no symptom that we are not living under a Conservative government. Allowing the general impoverishment, the upper classes are still living their accustomed life."[21] The government was caught in the age-old political trap of overpromising and underdelivering, because, in Orwell's view, the kinds of promises it had made lacked the necessary substance required to effect real change.

Nonetheless, Orwell also remained anxious that the second fate remained a medium-term possibility for Britain, especially if the Left intelligentsia could not be persuaded to abandon their faith in the good conduct of the USSR. That is why he set his final and bleakest novel, *Nineteen Eighty-Four,* not in the Soviet Union but in the UK. In that book, he took his argument to its absolutely worst possible conclusion. It was a paradoxically abstract novel about the evils of abstraction. But its driving force remained the same. If we allow our political leaders to develop a language detached from reality without fighting back, then over time we ourselves will lose the ability to conceptualize any real alternatives.

The most striking difference between *Nineteen Eighty-Four* and what had gone before, however, was the hopelessness with which Orwell now infused his narrative. Gone were the "dirty and ridiculous" but fundamentally "decent" human beings whom Orwell had previously determined made our societies what they are, replaced by the control of the inner party and two separate oppressed classes, the outer party, whose thoughts are directly monitored and controlled by their political masters, and the proles, who are so fundamentally worthless as to pose no effective challenge to the inner party's rule.[22]

The depth of pessimism in *Nineteen Eighty-Four* has perplexed Orwell's readers for generations since. Raymond Williams, writing in the Thatcher years, could not understand how Orwell had suddenly lost all faith in the ability of everyday people to use their everyday feelings, experiences, and memories to at least attempt to shrug off the oppressive control of Big Brother. Surely, the very capacity for resistance with which Orwell had endowed his everyday hero George Bowling in *Coming Up for Air* should have been available for Winston Smith in *Nineteen Eighty-Four*. In the earlier book, Bowling had seen through all of the lies, the grandiosity, and the danger of those who would oppress him by returning in his imagination to the so very real environment of his childhood. Winston Smith tries to recapture such a sense, longing for beauty and memory, but is afforded no such chance. For him, only the possibility of romantic love offers a plausible route to escape, but even that is left in tatters of defeat. It was, Williams concluded, "a dreadful underestimate" of the capacities of ordinary people to resist with recourse to the resources all around them.[23]

Other critics, such as Bernard Crick, have detected more glimmers of possibility in *Nineteen Eighty-Four*. Crick points out that the proles, for all their identification as an unthinking, apathetic mass, are briefly described as having "stayed human" by virtue of remaining committed to their "individual relationships" and understanding that a "gesture, an embrace, a tear, a word spoken to a dying man" can each have "value in itself." The proles, too, are immune to the powers of abstraction. They are "not loyal to a party or a country or to an idea" but only "loyal to one another." The proles lack agency, falling into a stereotype of the apathetic mass that echoes the worst aspects of Priestley's and Orwell's social reportage from the 1930s, but here there was at least as small reminder of what Orwell had used to believe could "humanize" our politics.[24]

Whatever the precise balance of pessimism and optimism in the book, however, by the time Orwell wrote *Nineteen Eighty-Four*, he had all but given up on the imminent possibility of an alternative politics. The future was either capitalist oppression or collectivist oppression, with great evils hidden from view by grandiose political rhetoric, and where people fail to think and act in terms of real, concrete realities instead. If anything could have saved the world from that end, Orwell recognized, it would have been the call of the everyday on ordinary people. Such a call could have acted as a reminder that, whatever politicians claim, there remain some realities that deserve celebration and preservation and other realities on which we can concretely act and improve. But whatever hope he might have once had that such a call would be loud enough to prevent the collapse into oppression, it had perished before he died.

One week after the election of Attlee's government was announced, Dylan Thomas sat down in the front room of the small flat he was living in in London's Markham Square to begin writing one of his most celebrated short stories. It was broadcast a few months later as "Memories of Christmas." For all of the promise of change around him, all of this obsession with the new, Thomas wrote a tale that drew its inspiration from the humane warmth of memory and from the repetition of customs and traditions across the ages. "One Christmas was so much like another," it opened. "I can never remember whether it snowed for six days and six nights when I was twelve or whether it snowed for twelve days and twelve nights when I was six," the story continued, before looking back on the day "we tobogganed down the seaward hill, all the afternoon, on the best tea tray and Mrs Griffiths complained, and we threw a snowball at her niece, and my hands burned so, with the heat and the cold, when I held them in front of the fire, that I cried for twenty minutes and then had some jelly."[25]

Thomas's Christmas story was no *Animal Farm* or *Nineteen Eighty-Four*. But it nonetheless issued an unmistakeable rebuke to the relentless march of progress all around him. On the surface, the message was simple: change must not come to Christmas. Its special wonder lies in its unchanging repetition and its escape from the tides of history, which we had to take care to protect. But its underlying meaning was deeper still. Britain must not become the kind of country where these continuities did not matter, where we turned our back on the everyday experiences that people care about most of all, in our headlong rush to secure far-reaching social change.

Again, like Orwell, none of this meant that Thomas wanted every-thing to stay the way it was. He did not. "The day will come when the old Dis-Order changeth, yielding to a new Order," he wrote to Pamela Hansford Johnson back in the early 1930s. The chances of ordinary people in Britain, he continued, were "being strangled . . . by the legion of old Buffers . . . clinging for God and capital to an out-grown and decaying system." The "capitalists and industrialists" are "grinding into power the bones and guts" of his generation, he con-cluded, and they had to be stopped. But, just like Orwell, he remained frightened throughout his life at the forces of oppression ranged around him. "Everything is wrong," his letter to Johnson continued. "The governments are wrong because they are committees of prohibi-tors; the presses are wrong, because they feed us what they desire to feed us, and not what we desire to eat; the churches are wrong, because they standardize our god, because they label our morals, because they laud the death of a vanished Christ, and fear the crying of a new Christ in the wilderness."[26]

Throughout his life, of course, innumerable friends and colleagues tried to tempt Thomas to affiliate to their causes. Marxists, anarchists, Welsh nationalists, mainstream socialists, all pressed their case, some-times over many months, but each without success. Probably the friend who came closest was Henry Teece, who led the frighteningly named Apocalyptic movement, inspired by D. H. Lawrence's last book, *Apocalypse*. Teece pressed hard in his efforts to tempt Thomas to join the fold, clearly believing that their shared love of Lawrence would be enough to seal the deal. But even here, Thomas resisted fairly straightforwardly. "I agree with and like" much of the *Apoca-lyptic Manifesto*, he wrote to Teece in 1938, but "I won't sign [it], with or without argument." "I wouldn't sign any manifesto unless I had written every word of it," he continued, "and then I might be too ashamed. . . . The language of such documents is strange to me."[27]

This reflection on the language of political manifestos shows that part of Thomas's disdain for political engagement came, like Orwell's, from his hatred of the grandiose abstract terminology that was favoured by politicians. "I always feel that one should be very reluctant of putting down any abstract words at all," Thomas advised in 1946, and he would have shuddered to have been associated with the sort of phrasing that flooded through documents like *Let Us Face the Future*.[28] But his primary resistance to conventional politics was not grounded in language, but from a lifelong hatred of bureaucracy. That hatred was partly personal. Thomas led a chaotic and disorderly life and often found himself falling foul of rules and regulations, especially as they concerned money. "An income tax form flops through the window, the letterbox is choked up with dockleaves. Let's get out, let's get out," he wrote to Oscar Williams in 1945.[29] But more than that, he hated what bureaucracy did to the human spirit, and especially the way it trampled over that which was held most dearly by people who possessed little power.

Thomas explored this theme most explicitly in a brilliant short radio play called *The Londoner,* recorded for the BBC one year into the Attlee government in 1946. The play focused on a working-class family who lived in Monrose Street, in London's Shepherd's Bush. The family are shown recovering from the war and reflecting on their future together in the context of the seemingly boundless social reform going on all around them. It contains reflections on the changing relationship between the generations, the decline of public spaces, the nuclear arms race, and the desperate search for economic security. Most of all, though, it is a play about power. It reflects, that is, on the ways in which the opinions and experiences of ordinary people are of no real interest to those who occupy high office and encourages the listener to think about the consequences. One small exchange near the beginning sets the tone to perfection:

Questioner: And what is Montrose Street? What does it look like?
Voice of an Expert: It is a grey-bricked street of one hundred houses. Built in 1890. Two bedrooms, a front room and a kitchen. Bathrooms were built into less than half of the houses in 1912.

A scullery and a backyard. Rent 28 shillings. Too cold in the winter, too hot in the summer. Ugly, inconvenient, and infinitely depressing.
Voice of an Old Resident: No, no. You got it all wrong. It's a nice, lively street. There's all the shops you want at one end, and there's pubs at both ends. Mightn't be much to look at, but there's always things going on, there's always something to see, buses and trams and lorries and prams and kids and dogs and dogfights sometimes and . . . [30]

It was in this context that Thomas began writing another radio play, the one that was to become his masterpiece, *Under Milk Wood*. At first blush, there was nothing very political at all about that new work, and it is hardly, if ever, read as a political treatise today. It tells the story of a single day in the life of a small imaginary Welsh seaside town, Llareggub, based on the village of Laugharne, where Thomas always felt happiest, most settled, and most creative. There are no holders of high office in the story, no officials, no inspectors, no one who really even enjoys a position of particularly high status, with the possible exception of the old sea captain, Captain Cat, and the Reverend who runs the town chapel, both of whom enjoy no real position of power over the other inhabitants. But with just a little reflection, it is not difficult to see that that is the point.

Under Milk Wood is Thomas's utopia, his final and most perfect effort to capture the world as it should be. It is not a utopia like that in the final part of *Gulliver's Travels* or that in Aldous Huxley's *Brave New World*, of course. It is not, that is, constructed through a process of abstraction that strips away the concrete and particular details of life in the hope of grasping something grand and generalizable, something of what the philosopher Immanuel Kant called the universal or the noumenal realm. Instead, it is constructed through a process of concentration. It zooms in on the details of life as closely as it can, in the hope of revealing that which is profound. With *Under Milk*

Wood, Thomas wanted to give listeners the direct experience of being somewhere specific, feeling its rhythms of life beat on their souls as the waves at the play's start beat on the shore. And he wanted to show that each of the elements of perfection to be found there comes not from the imagination of some grand theorist or from the aspirational dreams of some political movement but from the ordinary reality of today. *Under Milk Wood* is, in other words, a utopia of the everyday, where the magical and the parochial are as one, with all of the paradoxes that involves.

As Thomas came close to completing *Under Milk Wood,* in 1951, he wrote to his patron, Madame Caetani, to tell her excitedly all about this "longish play, as yet untitled, in verse and prose which I have been thinking of for a long time." He imagined it would appear to others as "gay and sad and sentimental and a bit barmy," but he felt its importance clearly and wanted her to see it.[31] *Under Milk Wood,* he wrote, would reveal a whole town of "eccentrics" who are both "ordinary and good." It would do so by journeying through

all the activities of the morning town—seen from a number of eyes, heard from a number of voices—through the long, lazy lyrical afternoon, through the multifariously busy little town evening of meals and drinks and loves and quarrels and dreams and wishes, into the night and the slowing-down lull again and the repetition of the first word: Silence. And by that time, I hope to make you utterly familiar with the places and the people; the pieces of the town will fit together; the reasons for all these behaviours (so far hinted at) will be made apparent; and there the town will be laid alive before you. And only you will know it.[32]

One of the most important characters listeners will come across in this journey, he continued, is a woman who shouts out into the street each morning because she "believes the town is the chosen land, and the little river Dewi the river of Jordan." "She is not at all mad," Thomas concluded, "she merely believes in heaven on earth."[33]

Heaven on earth was Thomas's perfect description of his utopia: a state that is already present to us but which we all overlook because we do not believe that something so ordinary can also be something so important.

At the risk of being overly schematic, this utopia had four component elements to it. It started with that countercultural love for the past for which Thomas was most renowned. The rhythm and repetition of the ages, along with the power of memory and reflection, are crucial in *Under Milk Wood*. The play's narrator makes that immediately clear. Taking the voice of a tourist guidebook, he says of Llareggub that "though there is little to attract the hill-climber, the health-seeker, the sportsman, or the week-ending motorist, the contemplative may . . . find, in its cobbled streets and its little fishing harbour, in its several curious customs, and in the conversation of its local characters, some of that picturesque sense of the past so frequently lacking in towns and villages that have kept more abreast of the times."[34] The first real character we meet is the blind former sea captain, Captain Cat, talking in his dreams to lost comrades, remembering the small things of life from the watery depths.

As always, the past celebrated is far removed from the glorious past of the establishment or the traditional story of the British nation-state. There is nothing grand here. Instead, it is the connection of the generations through everyday experience that holds the town together, not the established hierarchies or conventional behaviours. The singing Reverend Jenkins compares the town's natural beauty with its more celebrated neighbours:

> By mountains where King Arthur dreams
> By Penmaen Mawr defiant
> *Llareggub Hill* a molehill seems
> A pygmy to a giant[35]

The guidebook continues by informing us that "the one place of worship" in the town, "with its neglected graveyard, is of no architectural interest." The townspeople cannot even be bothered to take care of the graveyard. Moreover, the play continually insists on bringing any grandiose histories that do creep in back down to earth. At one moment, the narrator describes the scene on top of the hill overlooking Llareggub. "Stand on this hill," he says. "This is Llareggub Hill, old as the hills, high, cool, and green," and atop it is a "small circle of stones, made not by druids but by Mrs Beynon's Billy."[36] What matters in Llareggub are the people of the town themselves. Over the generations, they have shaped their own environment, and they continue to invest it with a kind of magic, while all the same returning again and again to timeworn conversations, expectations, and relationships.

The second utopian element of Thomas's Llareggub is the harmony of its community. The depth of community connectedness is everywhere in *Under Milk Wood*, explained in a fashion reminiscent of the great early twentieth-century sociologist Emile Durkheim. Durkheim had spoken of the "organic" connection between individuals who occupy different roles but each of whom is dependent on another, and that's precisely the form Thomas shows here. The narrator first introduces the characters by describing their trades or vocations, picturing as he does a harmony emergent from everyone's individual dependence on everyone else. "Hush, the babies are sleeping," the narrator begins, as are "the farmers, the fishers, the tradesmen and pensioners, cobbler, schoolteacher, postman and publican, the undertaker and the fancy woman, drunkard, dressmaker, preacher, policeman, the webfoot cocklewomen and the tidy wives."[37] No one competes with anyone else for any role or social purpose in Llareggub. They may not be entirely satisfied with their lot, and they may idly dream of new lovers or a life on their own, but they recognize each other, identify with their own role, and are conscious of their place within a complex whole that demands that they all play their parts, however begrudgingly or unsatisfactorily they do so. There is no competition for status, no striving after material success, no desire to do any other down, no desire to stand alone.

The third feature reinforces this theme. Llareggub is a distinctly anarchic utopia. There is a complete absence of asserted power in the town. No one instructs anyone, no one keeps harmony or an illusion of harmony together by insisting on it. Llareggub is as far removed from *Nineteen Eighty-Four* as it is possible to be. There are no police, no politicians, no bureaucracy, and certainly no informers. There is not even anyone like Miss La Trobe in Virginia Woolf's *Between the Acts* whose role it is to engender an artificial feeling of unity in a world that might otherwise come apart. Not even the town's chapel plays that part. Instead, the town copes perfectly well without any form of authority. Its rhythms and routines provide all the stability that is required.

This absence of authority is all the more noticeable because the residents of Llareggub are not natural conformists. In fact, they each possess what Thomas called a "salty individuality of their own."[38] This is the fourth utopian element of Thomas's town. Through the play's device of leaping from voice to voice, the listener cruises through the town, visiting each of the many people within it, gaining an acute sense of the inhabitants' differences as well as their similarities. Thomas himself noted that this rendered the play "rather jerky and confusing, with far too many characters and changes of pitch and temper."[39] But he believed nonetheless that the discordant voices found harmonious rhythm as they expressed the habits and practices of their everyday.

And that is precisely what the experience of listening to *Under Milk Wood* is like. It is hard initially to know what is going on or why, to work out which characters to invest in and which to overlook. But slowly it begins to become clear. It is the rhythm that matters, and the familiarity, the sense of a community coming together by doing what it always does, without instruction or compulsion, without grandiosity or plan. Just as Thomas had promised, Laugharne—or Llareggub—was heaven on earth, and a very earthly heaven it was too. And how can you not love it? Anyone pretending otherwise was surely just in envious denial. As Thomas himself said,

> They envy Laugharne its minding its own, strange, business; its sane disregard for haste; its generous acceptance of the follies of others, having so many, ripe and piping of its own; its insular, featherbed air; its philosophy of "It will all be the same in a hundred years' time." They deplore its right to be, in their eyes, so wrong, and to enjoy it so much as well. And, through envy and indignation, they label it and libel it a legendary lazy little black-magical bedlam by the sea. And is it? Of course not. I hope.[40]

Thomas's *Under Milk Wood* brilliantly distilled the essential elements of the public philosophy he and others had been creating since the 1930s. It reminded its listeners to preserve the best of the past even if they were striving for a better future; it gave them hope in the spirit of community; it reinforced the suspicion of bureaucracy, or of organized power of any sort; and it told us again to treasure the peculiarities, eccentricities, and diversities of ordinary people and not to worry that they would cause the whole social order to come tumbling down.

Each of these elements was, of course, a powerful rebuke to conventional politics, including Britain's politics under Attlee. If *Under Milk Wood* did not have Orwell's Thought Police, neither did it have the benign experts and social planners who were the essence of Britain after the war. There was no one here who would be interested in building a New Jerusalem, let alone anyone who thought that the way to do it was with a plan drawn up by technical experts beavering away in offices miles away in Whitehall. But what did it actually say about an alternative? What was anyone meant to do differently to make a world where there could be more Laugharnes, or at least where those that there were did not fall apart?

Thomas himself never answered these questions, or at least not directly. Perhaps because he couldn't. But the outline of the answer was now at least crystal clear. Any alternative could not be a politics driven by the central state. It had to be a politics of ordinary people. Nor could it be a politics driven by an obsession with economics, even the kind of economics that pursues greater equality. It had to be a politics centred in real relationships between people and their memories of the past. A politics, in other words, grounded in the humane aspects of everyday life, comfortable with emotion and sentiment and attachments to place, not embarrassed by them.

It was, in all likelihood, a politics that Thomas thought he would never see realized in actual form. Certainly, Orwell had given up hope. But then, out of nowhere, Thomas was surprised. For just as he was labouring away on the text of Under Milk Wood in 1951, he received an unwanted commission from the BBC to go up to London's South Bank to write a review of the newly opened Festival of Britain. He was reluctant. Official, government-sponsored festivals weren't really his thing, and this one, the last hurrah of Attlee's reforming government, looked on paper like everything he disliked most. It was a newly designed hygienic social environment, created on a bulldozed site on the side of the Thames by expert planners to give ordinary people a sense of what they could have if they were lucky enough, did what they were told, and didn't rock the boat. It was all concrete and shiny steel and full of the kind of improving exhibits that the well-meaning imagine that everyone else must have a lot to learn from even if they were a little dull. But, needing the money, he went. And then he changed his mind. For as he stood in the "brief city" of the festival site, not only did his anger ease, but the "furthest pinnacle" his worldview ever reached came into grasp.

6

Brief City

WHEN I WAS A CHILD, I went on holiday every year with my mum, dad, and sister Anna to the small Welsh seaside town of Aberaeron, just a few miles from where Dylan Thomas had lived forty years earlier. Each July, we stayed for a week in a caravan owned by my school history teacher. I remember the long, sticky, hot days as if they were yesterday. There were mornings spent dangling a line off the harbour wall trying to catch crabs and ending up with eels. There were afternoon walks along the front to the honey ice cream shop and short visits to the tiny sea life aquarium, with its spotted dogfish and prawns. And there was time just listening to the ringing of the bells on the boats as they bobbed up and down on the water.

What I remember most was a game we used to play with my mum, in the evenings, just as darkness fell outside. We would walk in the town and carefully peek, just quickly, through the windows of people's homes. We would see families sitting around the television and the dining table. We would see old men sitting off on their own reading the newspaper. We would see earnest women writing letters. We would see kids—probably the same age as me—lying on the floor with a comic or a game. Every house we went past was different. Wallpaper, decorations, photos on the mantelpiece. And yet almost every house was the same too. People living their lives according to a rhythm that they knew, a pattern that offered some reassurance to existence.

I thought about this game a lot as I went around the country in the Labour Party's battle bus during the general election of 2015. On the surface of it, an election campaign was a bit like my childhood game. The people of the country briefly making their private views public, and the politicians checking in on each of them. But were any of our politicians looking through those windows on that campaign? Were they genuinely listening when people talked? Of course they weren't. Everything was microtargeted Facebook ads, photo opportunities with lethargic-looking teenaged activists representing "youth," "town halls" with preselected campaign staff and the avoidance of any difficulty. The divorce between our professional politicians and everyday people and their concerns was never more apparent to me than on the campaign, with each side relentlessly rehearsing its focus-grouped messages and the public looking on bemused.

The great political scientist Peter Mair wrote an outstanding book about all of this in 2013, *Ruling the Void*.[1] I read it just as the 2015 campaign was beginning, and although I forget who gave it to me, I remember sharing passages of it with my Labour colleague Stewart Wood over text message. "There is a world of the citizens—or a host of political worlds of the citizens," Mair wrote and I paraphrased, "and a world of the politicians and the parties, and the interactions between them steadily diminishes. Citizens change from participants into spectators, while the elites win more and more space in which to pursue their own particular interests."[2]

The one mistake Mair made was to think that this was somehow new. In fact, Thomas and his colleagues felt the same in 1951 as Wood and I did in 2015. *Under Milk Wood*, I now realize, was a far more sophisticated version of my childhood game brought face-to-face with political reality. Here were the voices of the people, their hopes, dreams, terrors, excitements, laid out in plain view, just waiting for someone in power to take notice, but with the expectation that no one ever would.

Back in 1951, though, all was not lost. There was hope then, in a way there often feels there isn't anymore. And that's because the ideas that Thomas, J. B. Priestley, George Orwell, and others articulated had seeped far more fully into the national consciousness than they anticipated. The belief in the extraordinary power of ordinary people, the need to cherish the everyday habits and traditions of the past, to protect the small, the local, and the particular against the grand, the national, and the abstract, never gained full ideological supremacy, of course. It was buffeted always by Labour's new belief in the benign rule of experts and by the Conservative establishment's remaining faith in grand, imperial prestige. But it was there nonetheless, a serious, important, unavoidable rebuke to those who would ignore it and a spur to action to those it excited.

Nowhere was its influence more powerful than in the great Festival of Britain of 1951, the last year of Clement Attlee's government. Conceived as a way of celebrating the country's victory in the war, setting a path for the future, and possibly stimulating the economy along the way, the festival was an enormous undertaking for a country still only partially recovered from war. In London alone, there were two large sites, one on the South Bank of the Thames almost directly opposite the Houses of Parliament and one just a little farther downriver in Battersea, as well as art exhibitions in Whitechapel, scientific shows in South Kensington, and a living, ideal community in the East End. Elsewhere, there were major exhibits in Glasgow, Belfast, and Cardiff and a Royal Navy carrier, the *Campania*, that travelled the entire length of the coast, docking in port towns to help them mark the occasion. Almost every town and village in the country had a festival commemoration of some kind, whether involving the re-opening of a community centre, the dedication of a park, or the launch of a new local housing plan. Festival buses even drove around continental Europe bringing the essence of the celebration to recently liberated towns and cities. By the time it closed, close to nine million people had visited the London activities alone.

Every political, intellectual, and cultural grouping in Britain jostled to get control of the festival, and no one group prevailed entirely. Nonetheless, almost everything that has been explored over the previous five chapters found its place. There was a public commitment to community, understood as the ability of memory to tie people together even when they were unknown to each other, and freedom, understood as founded on local particularity and eccentricity. There was an attack on the overly grand expectations of both the traditional establishment and the new bureaucracy, with much lighthearted mockery of both a feature of many an event. And most of all, there was a big, bold celebration of the ordinary and the everyday as the heart of everything that was good about Britain. "Other demonstrations here and abroad have shown a country's art, its industries or its institutions, but none has tried like this to recreate a people's personality from birth to maturity," the festival's official guide put it. "This we shall not do by any system of abstractions, but by letting the work of British men and women, past and present, give evidence of their belief and purpose."[3]

The Festival of Britain began in the most unlikely way. In 1945, Gerald Barry, the editor of the *News Chronicle*, a mainstream Liberal newspaper, remembered that 1951 would be the centenary of Victoria and Albert's Great Exhibition. He immediately wrote an open letter to the president of the Board of Trade, Sir Stafford Cripps, suggesting that the time might be right for Britain to prepare a new exhibition. Such an exhibition, Barry explained, could provide the incoming government with the chance to "give an imaginative lead to the nation and the Empire."[4] Unsurprisingly, Cripps and his Labour colleagues were enormously flattered. It was an excellent idea. Such an exhibition could be a way to represent the achievements of the new government to the country and the world, to celebrate the victory in the war, and possibly to make a little money along the way. With remarkably little pause or debate, the notion was accepted in principle, followed by a short committee inquiry under the auspices of the Board of Trade, and a formal announcement to Parliament in December 1947. The Festival of Britain Office was established at the heart of government, all the political parties pledged their support, and Barry himself was appointed its director general, with just over three years to plan and deliver something that could rival the success of the Crystal Palace.

On the surface, the festival preparations that followed looked like an entirely nightmarish combination of the new socialist central planning and an old British establishment fix-up. The government appointed a Festival Council, chaired by General Lord Ismay, onetime chief of staff to Winston Churchill, and including the doyen of the new town-planning movement, Sir Patrick Abercrombie, alongside that bastion of the conservative belief in authority, T. S. Eliot. Of the council's twenty-nine other members, four were from the House of Lords, eleven were knights, eight were privy councillors, and only three were women. There were no representatives from the radical side of politics, the arts, or industry, and no one who plausibly represented or felt directly accountable to the ordinary people of Britain.

At cabinet level, the whole business was overseen initially by Cripps as president of the Board of Trade and then later, and very actively, by Herbert Morrison, whose formal title of lord president of the council often gave way to "Lord Festival." Morrison's special talent was the construction of public committees, councils, and corporations.

His primary task in government had been to design a model to run the newly nationalized industries, which involved as much input by experts and as little input by anyone else as possible. It was no surprise, then, that the festival was soon overrun by such agencies. The newly created Arts Council of Great Britain commissioned all of the visual arts. There was a Council for Science, which governed the creation of scientific exhibits both on the main site and in the new Museum for Science in South Kensington. There was a Council for Architecture, Town Planning and Building Research, which oversaw the physical design of the festival site and aimed to derive lessons from its architecture for future public projects. And there were festival committees for Scotland, Wales, and Northern Ireland, each with its own subcommittees and byzantine bureaucratic order.[5]

These government bodies did not just provide the overall direction for the festival, they were intended to drive most of the festival's day-to-day operations too, alongside a plethora of other existing government departments, of course. Catering on the main festival site on London's South Bank was to be overseen by the Ministry of Food, which regulated the thirteen cafés and restaurants and made special plans to ensure that foodstuffs otherwise unavailable because of rationing could be enjoyed by its visitors, even though visitors still had to hand in their ration coupons in order to buy any food.[6] And, of course, they aspired to govern everything in their own inimitably improving style. The main festival sites on the South Bank and in the East End were intended to be practical, lived examples of the advantages of a clean, orderly, well-constructed, and coherently planned age.

The dominance of Morrison's committees effectively did for any chance that Conservative messaging would be central to the festival, whatever Lord Ismay might have wanted. The festival could have been grand, bombastic, and exclusive, with a focus on the martial achievements of the British Empire or on narrow and prescriptive accounts of "good behaviour" and the British character. Most nineteenth- and early twentieth-century political celebrations had been of exactly this sort.[7] But Morrison and his colleagues would have none of that. They squashed any chance of the festival doing anything to echo the imperial grandeur of the 1851 Great Exhibition. Gone too were any echoes of the 1924 British Empire Exhibition, which had celebrated Britain's military prowess, its dominion of other nations, and the historic glories of its formal system of government: "the might, dignity, power and prestige of the Empire."[8] By the time the festival opened, there was not even any place for international trade, the idea that had initially spawned the interest.

In its place, at first blush, it looked as if the festival would be the socialist town-planning movement promised in *Let Us Face the Future* unleashed. Having been hampered for decades by political compromises and complex social realities, perhaps the festival could give the new generation of planners free rein to build as they thought fit? The festival could finally show British citizens that "a well-designed town is part of [their] wealth."[9]

Sure enough, there was a relentless modernism about the festival's main site on the South Bank. Its most striking building was the Dome of Discovery, a vast saucer-shaped structure, which was at the time the largest domed building in the world. It was accompanied by the Skylon, a huge, silver, rocket-like structure that appeared to hang effortlessly in the air.[10] The site's mastermind, the architect Hugh Casson, told the Arts Council's official magazine, *Image,* that the whole endeavour was a chance to "get architect and painters, engineer, landscape designer and sculptor working together in the same language" and for the public good.[11] And indeed, everything was taken care of on the festival's South Bank site by benign, well-informed experts, free of the chaos of commercial imperative or historic tradition. There were even "bins for nice people to put their paper in," Casson noted, an innovation unheard of in most British cities in wartime. "The things that one was expected to admire were the novelties," the historian Raphael Samuel recalled decades later.

"The bright new towns of the future . . . the clean lines of 'functional' architecture; the gay colours of 'contemporary' style."[12]

Despite all of this, neither Casson nor James Gardner, who was in charge of design at the second major London site at Battersea Park, was a straightforward disciple of the Labour government's reformist modernism. They were both too sceptical of the hold of bureaucracy for that. Nor would they have enjoyed total sway over festival planning even if they were. Such was the size of the festival endeavour that almost without Morrison noticing, a whole host of other up-and-coming architects, artists, designers, journalists, and poets were recruited to the ranks of festival organizers, charged individually with curating one small section or another of the festival, and also with working together in the festival's office in London's Savoy Court to shape the overall feel and purpose of the event.

Among them were staunch opponents of the new order and clear disciples of the tradition described in this book. Laurie Lee, for one, was hired both to write the captions that visitors would read at the exhibits on the major site on the South Bank and to curate an exhibition on "eccentricity" for a pavilion examining the British national character. Also, there was Barbara Jones, who had been employed alongside John Piper in the war to record a disappearing England in paint and ink and had developed in the process an unrivalled understanding of the painting and craft produced by ordinary people across the country. Jones was asked to re-create the English seaside on the South Bank site and to organize the first official celebration of "British popular and traditional art" at the festival's takeover of Whitechapel Art Gallery.[13]

With all of their influence and direction and almost without anyone noticing, the official purpose of the festival changed to include a whole host of the themes central to this book. By the time the Festival of Britain opened in May 1951, its official theme was to provide "the autobiography of a nation," and to do so with particular emphasis on "our standards in the arts and in design, our integrity and imagination in the sciences and in industry, the values—personal and collective—which have designed and now operate in society."[14] In order to do so, it trumpeted three themes in particular: the place of everyday pleasure in British life, the pull of the past in British self-identity, and the need to preserve the parochial in a nationalizing age. As they sought to tell the story of Britain, sometimes it looked as if the festival organizers had used Orwell's *Lion and the Unicorn* as their guide.

It all started with pleasure. Asked at its opening by the *Daily Mail* to describe what the festival was really all about, Gerald Barry said it was designed to evoke the British spirit of "fun and enthusiasm." Some, he continued, would even call it an "austerity binge."[15] As such, the South Bank site was designed most of all to stimulate the senses. "Young people especially were inspired by the colour and the texture, the glass and metal structures, the floodlighting and the instant landscape with fountains and lakes wherever you looked," Casson recalled.[16] There was a dancing pavilion, sound and music shows, even the world's biggest television. It was no coincidence that the most striking—and most popular—structure on the South Bank site, the Skylon, had no practical purpose. It was just there.[17]

For all of his modernist seriousness, Casson described his master plan for the South Bank as a "space for leisured gaiety, a place if you like for pleasure." It was a "gigantic toyshop for adults" intended to be "even a little mad."[18] No design opportunity was overlooked in the pursuit of this desire to provoke pleasure. "Outside" the festival site, "the soot and the smoke were in charge," Casson explained. Inside, the demands of industrial labour were not to be felt. In Casson's words, the festival's design had to provide an "inexplicable lift of heart" that would enable a "brief forgetting of office and factory."[19] To achieve such a result, the South Bank site itself was masked on the side that faced inland by a coloured screen of bright baubles and zig-zag shapes designed to obscure the bleak working world on the other side.

The waterfront was crucial too. The Thames had not been seen from this side for many generations, blocked out by the Lion Brewery and a series of warehouses and factories. They built a fake beach alongside it, with imaginary seaside amusements and freak shows, and they even offered sticks of rock with "South Bank 1951" running through them. The views across the river were also revealed in all of their fluid and watery glory, interrupted only by periodically explosive fountains, modelled on those at Versailles, which were designed to give a playful air to the excessively grand gothic of the Houses of Parliament across on the north bank.[20] Insofar as the South Bank was futuristic, it was not in the serious spirit of *Let Us Face the Future*. Rather, the South Bank site offered people a chance briefly to live out their *Dan Dare* comic fantasies, with its displays of rocket propulsion and the promise of new technological discoveries to come.

Dylan Thomas saw this as soon as he arrived to report on the festival for the BBC. There was nothing "shoddily cajoling" about the South Bank experience, Thomas explained. The South Bank was "gay, absurd, irrelevant, delighting imagination that flies and booms and spurts and trickles out of the whole bright boiling." The whole site was of this order, Thomas noted, from "the small stone oddity that squints at you round a sharp, daubed corner" to "the sexless abstract sculptures serenely and secretly existing out of time . . . that appear, but for one struck second, inappropriate." And watching the thousands of visitors explore the exhibits brought the point home to him more clearly still. "You see people go along, briskly down the wide white avenues towards the pavilion of their fancy—'Our Humbert's dead keen on seeing the milk-separators'—and then suddenly stop: another fancy swings or bubbles in front of their eyes. What is it they see? Small childbook-painted mobiles along the bridges that, at the flick of wind, become windmills and thrum round at night like rainbows with arms."[21]

More importantly, all of this meant that the South Bank was made by the people "without whom the exhibition could not exist, nor the country it trombones and floats." The most creative element of the South Bank, that is, came not from any formal elements of the architecture or design but from the experiences of those who visited the festival in their millions. As Thomas saw it, the people who mattered most were not the architects or the guides but ordinary visitors. He told the BBC that the festival succeeded because of

> the suspicious people over whose eyes no coloured Festival wool can possibly be pulled, the great undiddleable; they are the women who will not queue on any account and who smuggle in dyspeptic dogs; the strangely calculating men who think that the last pavilion must be the first because it is number twenty two; the people who believe they are somewhere else, and never find out that they are not . . . the vaguely persecuted people, always losing their gloves, who know that the only way they could *ever* get around would be to begin at the end, which they do not want to; people of militant individuality who proclaim their right to look at the damnfool place however they willy-nilly will.[22]

Even if the visitors were in charge, this was not an accident. As Casson said, the whole South Bank site was designed to ensure "everybody felt it was their show."[23] This was achieved by the relentlessly everyday and domestic focus of what went on. Sometimes, as the philosopher James Tully has it, pleasure in public life is celebrated for its ability to "liberate us from the routines of everyday life" and to create something wholly new.[24] But not here. The festival was not an escape from everyday life. It was everyday life. Just a little bit more so. The chief success of the Festival of Britain, therefore, lay in its ability to invite visitors to stay themselves, even to become a little bit more themselves by casting off some well-preserved inhibitions and restraints. They were, in other words, asked, encouraged, and enabled to explore their own sensibilities and celebrate their own desires, even

while they were also asked to glimpse the better future that democracy could bring. Here, citizens were able to keep to the rhythm of
their own lives, while also living them out against a backdrop more
expansive and more creative than they had ever seen before.

All of this explains why there was no off-putting grandeur on the
South Bank. No booming vistas. No processional walkways. Little evidence of monarchy. No empire. No glory. It was all proudly and relentless domestic. There was innovation and experimentation aplenty,
of course, but even it was very largely focused on improvements to
the actual, lived experience of British citizens of all backgrounds, not
on technical supremacy for the sake of it. There were new ways to
enjoy television, to save labour in the kitchen, to complete daily
chores at work, to relax in affordable comfort, and even to eat out-
doors, a practice previously unheard of in middle-class British society
and rendered all but impossible in the urban living spaces occupied
by the poor.[25] The South Bank "reinvented the city in the image of
the home," Alan Powers notes, "two categories which long-standing
convention had made strangers to each other."[26] In a further telling
example, when the Arts Council held a competition to find five paint-
ings to symbolize the festival, it chose some celebrated works—such
as Lucian Freud's *Interior in Paddington* and Patrick Heron's *Christmas
Eve*—but it also selected *Miss Lynn*, an image of an ordinary woman
reclining on a sofa by Claude Rogers of the Euston Road School. *Miss
Lynn* won simply because "she looked familiar," G. S. Whittet recalled. "Everybody knows a Miss Lynn."[27]

Sex played a vital part in this story too. The great world's fairs and
exhibitions of the previous century had often been sites where illicit
forms of sexualized entertainment received temporary official permis-
sion. And the festival was no exception. Some of this, it must be
said, was rather unimaginative. The Festival of Britain drew crowds
with its "gorgeous drum majorettes," who paraded many times a day,
and, more worryingly still, with a game called "Tip the Lady," which
saw young women in bathing suits balanced on stands until toppled

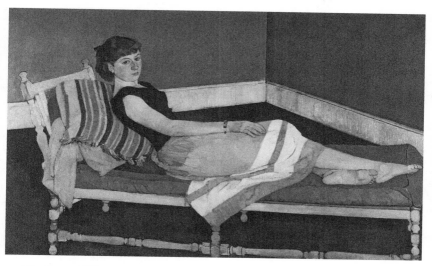

Miss Lynn, 1951
Southampton City Art Gallery, Hampshire, United Kingdom/Bridgeman Images

off into vats of water at the throw of a rubber ball. But more important were the ways in which visitors were encouraged to free themselves of at least a few of the many constraints of "proper conduct" at
the South Bank.[28] The site was open late into the night every day,
despite the expense of doing so at a time of severe resource shortages,
to encourage people to relax. Festival organizers even hired people
to pretend to be ordinary visitors and begin dancing each evening,
because they quickly learnt that the "English are too shy to dance in
public" without encouragement.[29]

That visitors took warmly to this prodding is widely recorded in
the enormous number of memoirs and autobiographical accounts
written since and was a topic of constant discussion in the coverage
provided by the contemporary press. A sense of liberation from the
more oppressive social mores was a clear attraction of a visit to the
festival site. There were festival affairs and marriages galore. But
the visitors' sense of ownership of the South Bank site did not rest on

romance or sex alone. As Thomas explained, thousands gave the site their own imprimatur, constantly reinventing it and having fun along the way. As one former festivalgoer, Wendy Bonus, remembers, as a nine-year-old, she got "lost in the Dome of Discovery," and that kind of says it all.[30]

All of this celebration and encouragement of everyday pleasure had a serious purpose. It was not just the result of some unconstrained hedonism, nor was it simply designed to cheer people up after the adversities of the war. Instead, it was intended as a fundamental part of a particularly British idea of freedom that it was the job of the festival to express.

This was seen most clearly in the "Lion and the Unicorn" pavilion on the South Bank, which set out to tell the story of both liberty and the British national character, and which was turned, with the help of Laurie Lee, who wrote the descriptive placards, into an unconstrained celebration of whimsical eccentricity. "We are the Lion and the Unicorn—twin symbols of the Briton's character," the exhibit began. "As a Lion, I give him solidity and strength. With the Unicorn, he lets himself go!" Visitors then saw a fantastic sculpture made of straw by the folk artist Fred Mizen of the Lion desperately trying to get the Unicorn to listen to him while the Unicorn flits away. After that, visitors to the pavilion walked past re-creations of some moments in the history of British liberty, including the signing of Magna Carta and a diorama of the Tolpuddle Martyrs, until they finally reached "eccentrics' corner," where they were told that the British "instinct of liberty" was best seen in the expressive diversity of its personalities, stretching from the village idiots of rural folklore to the wild and fantastic creations of Lewis Carroll.

Once again, much of this had come from ordinary people themselves. Lee had collected all of the contents of this "eccentrics' corner" in open houses in the festival's office in London's Savoy Place the year before. Responding to advertisements in the national press, long queues of men and women had stretched out from Lee's office door and run along the narrow corridor, with people clutching weird and wonderful objects, making the scene look to our modern eyes like a fairy-tale version of the *Antiques Roadshow*. Lee talked to each of these patient visitors in turn, examining their objects: a mandolin made of matchsticks, a tea set of fishbones, a "humane" mousetrap comprising a steel box doused with black pepper so that the mouse would sneeze itself to death.

Eccentricity, Lee always insisted to anyone who would listen, is one of the crucial characteristics of the British. It is the quality that ensures that Britain has never fallen prey either to utopian demagogues or to nihilistic pessimists. It is the quality that makes the country free. Reflecting on the festival's central purpose, Gerald Barry wrote that "in a world given over to violence it is important to show that a free nation still has a mind to the creative virtues, on which the health of any people must ultimately depend."[31] Lee put the same message at the end of the "Lion and the Unicorn" pavilion in his own distinctive idiom. "Hmm," the Unicorn was seen to say, the history of British character is "part earth . . . part cabbage."[32]

The whimsy of the "Lion and the Unicorn" pavilion illustrated a further element of the festival spirit: the nostalgic dedication to the popular past. For all of the high tech of the Dome of Discovery and the Skylon, the festival revelled most comfortably in days gone by. "The tavern, the music hall, the theatre, which have triumphantly survived, are links with an old Merrie England," J. B. Priestley told the *New York Times*, and by "bringing colour and light, pageantry and song, dance and drama, to scores of drab places," the festival "represents a breakthrough of the old spirit."[33] This centrality of the past was displayed most clearly in the exhibition curated by Barbara Jones at the Whitechapel Gallery in East London, which she called *Black Eyes and Lemonade*. The ostensible purpose of Jones's exhibition was to examine "the things people make for themselves or that are manufactured in their taste," but she turned it into a last-ditch effort to

save a host of popular artforms that she thought the rapidly modernizing country was in danger of losing forever.

In developing her argument, Jones was indebted like many festival
luminaries to Johan Huizinga. Just before the war, Huizinga had
written his widely praised *Homo Ludens*, insisting that "the play element" of everyday life "is declining in the face of scientism, adminis-
tration, routine, mass warfare and the professionalization of sports and
politics."[34] It was an argument that compelled a host of creative artists to act. Alongside fellow aficionados Margaret Lambert and Enid
Marx, Jones believed that "the 'innocent eye' is disappearing in
England," because of a whole combination of modernizing factors, including mechanical production, the erosion of traditional leisure,
the decline of villages and market towns, and the growth of metropolitan centres and the suburbs. Taken all together, these trends were
generating a "certain lack of initiative and interest in things with a
distinctive individual character." In such times, Lambert and Marx
explained, "we buy more from chain stores, the country craftsmen are
dying out and with them that individuality in design and decoration
that gave life to the old popular art."[35] Jones was more intemperate:
the "inevitable spoon-feeding of a mechanized system has coddled the
creative impetus out of almost everybody."[36]

Jones's belief in the importance of the historic art of everyday life
grew as she was completing a wartime commission to capture views
and vistas of a disappearing Britain for the Ministry of Information's
Recording Britain project. As she traipsed through the standard array
of thatched cottages, pretty parish churches, and grand country
houses, she was struck most of all by the everyday arts that she
came across, including shopfronts and signs, graveyard monuments,
children's toys, the decorations of boats and carts, carnival rides.
There was, she noted, a vast difference in style and taste between traditional craft designs for such everyday items and their new, mass-
produced equivalents. The traditional versions, she noted, were "florid
and startling to the fustian contemporary eye," with the most intri-

cate of twists and curls and almost baroque flourishes a common feature. Although not always easy on the eye, such art "makes so vivid an impression that we can easily forget how slender their hold on existence really is."[37]

In studying these objects closer, Jones identified three primary characteristics of this art that she came to believe made it preferable to its more orderly modern equivalent. First, it was complex, not simple, and as such revealed a depth of commitment to the artistic process quickly disappearing from ordinary lives. The lines were not clean, and the work took a long time to produce and required extraordinary levels of skill, patience, and practice. "Complexity," she reasoned, is "the legacy of illiteracy and a simple way of life; only those who cannot read and write remember long ballads, or elaborate smocking patterns; only those who live such a separate and lonely life as that of canal boatmen will create elaborate layers of decoration round their daily lives. The ever more fretful life of an ever-larger number of town dwellers has simplified the vernacular arts enormously—compare a Dodgem with a roundabout, a motor funeral with a horse one, liquorice all-sorts with candy floss."[38]

Second, the art was far more likely than its modern equivalent to grapple openly with fundamental questions of life and death, loss and heartbreak. There were displays of unremitting horror in some of the objects she collected, even from seemingly innocuous places like schoolyards, playgrounds, and parks. Here were people ravaged by illness or staring death in the face or mourning the loss of loved ones in some desperate accident. "Fear is concealed by sophisticated man, and today in any case he has less chance of it to express, as urban amenities are driving the dark edges round the cities further and further towards the sea," Jones explained. But with traditional arts, horror "appears suddenly in peaceful streets and fields, finding expression in Punch and Judy or the *Police Gazette*, in a ventriloquist's dummy, in sad architecture by riversides, in the little tents that house freaks at a fair."[39] The erosion of such art, she implied, was undermining a central element of the way that ordinary people deal with the extraordinarily unpleasant aspects of their lives. In the tidy, modern world of the benign welfare state, all of this was hidden away by well-meaning bureaucracy, leaving those who suffered at the hands of fortune unable to find straightforward public expression of their woe.

Third, and probably most importantly for Jones, she felt that these traditional arts pulsated with dynamic creativity and energy in a way sadly lacking from their modern equivalent. "One fact is constant through all the vernaculars: energy," she said. There was a sense in this art, she insisted, of a people making its own history, even if not in circumstances of their own making. The loss of this energy was, once again, a real harm visited on ordinary people by their supposed betters acting in their supposed interests. In contemporary society, Jones explained, this creative energy still exists, but it has to squeeze its expression into the small areas of life from which it is not repressed. "This energy lurks in the most vitiated of us," she explained, "displaying itself in elaborate hair-styles, well-polished shoes, or model-making; some of it only appears on suburban Sundays, diverted from creation to cleaning the car."[40] Jones's hope both for her own exhibition and for the festival at large was that it could remind people just how important this creative energy can be to all of our lives. The potential to develop it and explore it should not be locked up in universities and colleges of art reserved only for the elite, Jones insisted, but treasured throughout our life, especially in the everyday aspects that take most of our time and capture most of our attention.

The emphasis on the importance of this "zest for life" echoed Hugh Casson's and Gerald Barry's dedication to the promotion of pleasure on the South Bank site, of course, and was a dominant theme in all festival coverage. It was also found in another of the festival's crucial commitments: to the local and the parochial. Although the London events would capture most of the media's attention in 1951 and most of the attentions of historians since, the festival organizers were determined that it would be a celebration of localism at least as much as it was a celebration of the metropolis. Britain "was among the first to recognize and protect the freedom of individual towns," the official guide instructed, "and the form which the Festival of Britain has taken is a further proof [of] this ancient principle."[41] The festival, then, would have an event of some kind in almost every village and town across the whole country, and it was also celebrated in a series of books called *About Britain*, designed as "guides to the living Britain, covering the whole country . . . its scenery, its monuments, its buildings, its natural history, its people and their work and characteristics."[42]

More than localism alone, the festival was designed to deepen the parochial attachment of the British people to the places where they lived. Smallness was at the festival's heart. Local celebrations were, in other words, determinedly unremarkable and specific to the places in which they occurred. They were decidedly not designed to "raise the sights" of citizens to the heavens or to some future national glories, as had been the way of these sorts of events before. Instead, they were intended to remind people of how important their immediate surroundings were to the quality of their lives. The festival, the official guide thus continued, would be remembered in most communities for "repointing and repainting the Town Hall, gilding the church clock, for planting window boxes, flower baskets and temporary gardens, for painting the street lamps, decorating the streets and floodlighting the buildings."[43]

Nor was it all to be official-led either. The festival would not be shaped by the activities and the interests of councils and councillors, especially those who expressed some kind of ideological agenda or party allegiance. Instead, it was rooted in "the spontaneous expression" of the "life and interests" of everyday people. In some towns, the festival guide continued, the events of 1951 would be marked by "the flower show, the cricket week, fetes and dances, whist drives, musical and dramatic competitions or festivals, brass band contests, folk-dancing, gymkhanas and regattas, sheepdog trials."[44] It was a list that could have come directly out of Orwell's *Lion and the Unicorn*. J. B. Priestley himself captured the spirit perfectly in possibly his most parochial novel of all, *Festival at Farbridge*, which was, of course, written for the event itself.[45]

For all of the romance, all of the *Lion and the Unicorn* made real, none of this was straightforward in reality. There were tensions and ironies aplenty at the Festival of Britain. It displayed a localism and fondness for the parochial, but it was nonetheless organized by a plethora of official bodies in Whitehall. It placed a sentimental attachment to the past at its heart, but it also created modern architecture like the Dome of Discovery that had no parallel in the world at the time. It was intended as a celebration of the British people's desire to place pleasure before the constraints of officialdom, but for some it remained most of all a victory for planning. What is more, it had almost nothing to say about the injustices of Britain's imperial past or the decolonizing project of the present, and it rolled all of England, Wales, Scotland, and Northern Ireland's national histories into one, in a way that even seemed unconvincing at the time. Such wilful blindness stood in direct opposition to its stated mission of reflecting the country back to itself.

No tension, however, was greater than that between the state and the market. Although the festival site was designed as a celebration of the individualities of British character, that is, it was also intended to represent the triumph of a new economic order over the free rein of the market. The festival was an initiative for the public good that was to be overseen by the agents appointed and monitored by the government itself, uncontrolled, even uninfluenced, by the commercial demands of the market.

This ethos, so foreign to most twenty-first-century official eyes, was sacrosanct to the vast majority of festival organizers. Barry and Morrison insisted that the main festival exhibition on the South Bank eschew all commercial sponsorship. The market was not to be allowed to determine what the public saw, nor was it to shape the experience that they had whilst they visited the main festival grounds. As Barry insisted, "there was to be no space to let" on the South Bank. "No one would be able to get his goods exhibited by paying to do so; they would get there by merit or not at all."[46] Barry even insisted that the Festival of Britain's much-celebrated logo, designed by Abram Games, should not be restricted by copyright, but should rather be made freely available to all users, for adaptation and use in whatever way citizens thought fit.[47]

Festival organizers fought a tireless battle against commercial interests that wished to capitalize on the popular appeal of the festival. One bicycle company even tried to smuggle advertisements onto the site by hiding them on the side of a barge that had been bought by the South Bank's planners for the purpose of launching fireworks. Fortunately for Barry and Morrison's commercial-free vision, the eagle-eyed organizer of Festival River Spectacles, Antony Hippisley Coxe, noticed the suspicious canvas covering the posters on the side of the barge, revealing all before it could be put in place on the Thames.[48]

Even with such sterling efforts, this battle against private enterprise was far from entirely successful. Although the distinguished historian Kenneth Morgan once celebrated the absence of "tatty commercialism" from the festival, he could only do so by adopting astonishingly selective vision. In fact, the festival was swimming in tat.[49] There were postcards, souvenirs, magazines, and maps of all sorts produced to "celebrate" the festival by private firms interested more in making a profit than in edifying the nation and stimulating its communal creativity. There was also an astounding array of festival-inspired advertising. Open the official festival guide to the South Bank Exhibition, with its glorious Abram Games cover, and you were faced not by a crest or a powerful poem or a startling image of the nation's glories but by a full-page advert for Benedict's processed peas: "No other peas are quite the same, so ask for Benedict by the name."[50] As the festival presented "the story of the nation," one advertiser explained, so they offered "the story of the fountain pen," which was "the history of Waterman's." Another noted that "Dignity, Stability, and Durability" were the qualities of the British nation celebrated at the festival and were also the qualities of "Selleck, Nicholls, and Co. Builders in Concrete." One more suggested that the "Discovery of the Century" was the transformation of the "the Hinge of Today" into the "Hinge of Tomorrow." Finally, Bic, the makers of the Biro, modelled a celebratory pen after the festival's most famous landmark, the Skylon.[51]

Such a profusion of commercial advertising clearly diluted the image that the festival organizers aspired to, indicating that even in Attlee's Britain the market would always find a way to muscle in. The most serious challenge of all to the festival's vision of market-free space, though, came from inside the organization itself: the Battersea Pleasure Gardens. The gardens had been intended to be a complement to the South Bank, where enjoyment would continue, but in a setting more rural and less strikingly urban than the main festival site. But the plan unravelled almost from the start. Whereas everything else was run by the government councils and committees so favoured by Herbert Morrison, the gardens were run by a limited company, Festival Gardens Ltd, which was granted remarkably little financial support and operated with significantly less oversight.[52]

The resulting gardens destroyed the festival's efforts to keep the market at bay. Where the South Bank was proudly British, with its products and its exhibits extolling the possibilities of British technology put to work for the people, the pleasure gardens centred on features imported from outside. One of its highlights, the Big Dipper roller coaster, had to be bought at great expense in America, as apparently no one in Britain knew how to construct one.[53] But most importantly of all, whereas the South Bank site waged war against commercialism, the pleasure gardens were awash with it. Children were left at Nestle's playground, which offered not only "to look after children left in their care" but also to "give them a wee present when their parents came to collect them."[54] There were no prizes for guessing which chocolate manufacturer made the present, of course, or what the purpose of providing it really was. Visitors' memoirs report that the most popular exhibit of all was the Guinness Toucan clock, which aimed to show that all time is "Guinness time."

Many of the festival's organizers were dismayed by this not only because it undermined their efforts to put on a commercial-free endeavour but also because it directed attention towards a crucial difficulty at the very heart of their underlying vision. It was hard, after all, to celebrate the creativity and dynamism of the individual, as the festival organizers wished to do, without allowing free expression to the forms of creation that British individuals actually liked. And that is precisely why the commercialism muscled in yet again. For all the creative glories of the South Bank or of *Black Eyes and Lemonade*, it was the toucan clock and the Far Tottering and Oyster Creek miniature railway that just as truly represented the British at play. It was a dilemma that no one ever managed to resolve.[55]

This inability to constrain the market was one of the primary reasons why not everyone was impressed with the festival. "I expected something more spectacular," Stephen Spender later recalled. Spender wanted the whole social and economic order to be challenged in Attlee's Britain, a new dawn to rise, and as such he felt there was little to celebrate in "a material and spiritual phenomenon" characterized by "cut-rate cheerfulness cast in concrete and beflagged."[56] These kinds of criticism have long lived in academia. Even as the festival was remembered most fondly by the Victoria and Albert Museum at its twenty-fifth-anniversary celebrations, the historian Roy Strong took the opportunity of a foreword to its catalogue to lambaste the festival's failure to embrace big, bold, systemic change. "All references past or present to divisions of rich and poor, of class, of state as against private education, of state as opposed to private medicine were, of course, glossed over," Strong lamented, as officially it was nonpolitical.

This "vision was of harmony, of men and women heroically one, although descended from different stock."[57] It was naïve, storybook. Not a powerful political statement.

All of this is, of course, to wholly miss the point. The Festival of Britain wasn't an aggressive statement of political intent, designed to capture the spirit of *Let Us Face the Future*. Instead, it was the instantiation of an alternative idea. It was an official recognition that for all the change in the world—much of which was necessary and desirable—it was vital too to play tribute to the everyday, to recognize the rhythms and routines of ordinary people, the traditions that they treasured, the pleasures that they wished to pursue. Putting all that another way, the festival marked the domestication of the planning agenda of 1945. It was the moment that Attlee met the everyday. Gone was the heroic hubris of the government's early days. Arrived was a new spirit of normality. "The Festival style belongs firmly and squarely," Strong more persuasively said, "to the piazzas and pedestrian precincts, the espresso bars and community centres, to the blocks of council flats and rows of little houses."[58] There was improvement. There were new services. But there was nothing big, nothing grand, everything everyday. It was a moment when the world of officialdom and of politics looked through the windows of everyday people, liked what it saw, and mirrored it back to the world.

The festival could not last, of course. "If I had my way, I would keep central London illuminated in this glorious fashion for years and years," Priestley said.[59] But in fact, it all went almost as fast as it arrived. As the Attlee government fell and the Conservatives returned, the festival was all but wiped from existence. The South Bank site was demolished, with the exception of the Royal Festival Hall, to make way for a venue to celebrate the coronation of Elizabeth II, and the Battersea Pleasure Gardens sold off to the highest bidder. Some of the public art remained, but most towns and villages forgot their festival events. Barbara Jones's effort to rescue traditional, amateur artforms dropped off the nation's cultural agenda once again.

For some, the sense that it could not really last had always been integral to the very idea itself. Just as "Boxing Day ends Christmas with a litter of screwed paper, a doleful aftermath at one with the deserted fairground and the winter arcade," so the "impermanence" of the festival marked the comings and goings of life, the sense that love is always, at least eventually, accompanied by loss.[60] Melancholy was part of the everyday. Hiding away from the tragic elements of life, the sense of loss and disappointment, as well as the great joys of pleasure, was one of the pathologies of the modern that the festival aimed to correct. Pretending everything was going to be all right was not something you could ever blame Thomas or Orwell or Priestley for. It was right that the festival should embrace this sense of disappointment too.

For others, though, the loss was almost too much to bear. Many had a sense that this was an achievement that would not be repeated, a moment that marked the highest point of a way of thinking about the world. "This time last year when our Festival was flaunting its pretty gaiety," Marghanita Laski wrote on the anniversary of the festival's launch, "we knew already that far from marking a rung on the ladder of progress this might be the furthest pinnacle we could reach."[61] She was right. As Winston Churchill's government began to take the Dome of Discovery apart piece by piece in 1952, it was more than Hugh Casson's "brief city" that passed. A whole era had come to an end.

7

Acquaintance plus Wonder

A FEW YEARS AGO, I worked opposite the site of the old Festival of Britain, now called the South Bank, and I often used to walk there at lunchtime. There was much that was glorious there still. There were exhibition halls and concert halls, coffee bars and public art. There was an outdoor secondhand bookseller, an improvised skateboard park, and a heaving food market selling gourmet snacks the likes of which festivalgoers could only have dreamed. Of an evening, the lights sparkled just as J. B. Priestley wanted them to, and people from all different backgrounds, of all different ages, met, mingled, laughed, and made memories that could last a lifetime. But by the time I was there, much had changed. The Skylon was gone, the name appropriated by a sleek expense-account restaurant. Below, the front of the Royal Festival Hall, where Hugh Casson fought to remove all signs of commercialism almost seventy years ago, is now a panoply of chain restaurants. Just a few minutes up the river, the building that was the home of the London County Council now houses a McDonald's, a sandwich bar, and Shrek's Adventure!, an "interactive and immersive walkthrough experience, where the whole family can step into and star in your own hilarious misadventure with Shrek and his DreamWorks friends." It is a long way from *The Lion and the Unicorn*.[1]

In other words, a lot has changed since the festival closed its doors. In 1951, it was plausible to suggest that it represented the whole of the nation, or at least that the eyes of the nation moved to it to see how it was being represented. But not anymore. With the twin crises of Brexit and COVID-19, Britain now is riven by divisions unseen for generations, and central London, now a truly "global city," no longer represents the whole. Instead, on questions ranging from public health to immigration, from jobs to the foundations of the economy, London stands apart. It has little in common with the postindustrial English regions, blighted as so many of them are by desperate inequalities, economic decline, public service cutbacks, and a gnawing feeling of being ignored. The same is true of Wales. Scotland, meanwhile, edges ever closer towards full independence, with the Scottish National Party exerting a dominance entirely unpredicted only a few decades ago. Even the future of Northern Ireland within the union is at stake to a degree not witnessed since the 1920s. No one walks over Waterloo Bridge from the South Bank and looks up at the dome of St. Paul's nowadays and thinks of a nation united, facing the future, confident about its past.

The journey from 1951 to now has not been a linear one, of course. Britain has gone through periods of relative political stability and tension over the decades. The willingness of government to intervene in fundamental aspects of life has waxed and waned, and the power of commercial corporations has grown, fallen, and grown again. The overarching tendencies of the last few decades—the period some call neoliberalism—have been clear enough, though. Under the governments of Margaret Thatcher, John Major, Tony Blair, Gordon Brown, David Cameron, and Theresa May, there has been a retrenchment of the powers of central government in the economy and an increasing reliance on the market. This has led directly to growth both in the power of large corporations and in economic inequality, especially when it comes to the distribution of wealth. There is a reason that DreamWorks' Shrek ended up on the South Bank: only a brand of that size and a company of that wealth could afford to be there. And the consequences seep far wider and deeper than the South Bank. Even before COVID-19 laid the inequalities bare, a clear majority of people no longer believed that their children will have the economic opportunities that they enjoyed, nor did they believe that core public services—education, health, social insurance—will be there in the future to the same degree as they have been for them.

At the same time, there has been a rampant professionalization of party politics. There is now a closer affinity between most leading politicians and their equivalents at the top of big business than there is between politicians and the ordinary people whom they claim to represent, and public levels of trust in mainstream politics have collapsed as a result. To make everything worse, all of this is happening at the same time as a host of new challenges grow. Digital technology has already transformed political campaigning, opening Britain up to "fake news" and to the vicious polarization of Twitter; local newspapers have collapsed, alongside a host of other institutions that used to connect politics to the rhythms of everyday life, from local trade union branches to Church of England parish congregations. The institutions that Priestley celebrated as the heart of British democracy have decayed to the point of disappearance.

We all know where this has left the country. Millions of British people now report being deeply disenchanted by mainstream politics and its failure to protect public health, provide economic security, or even just offer a sense of being listened to and respected. And increasingly they are taking action. In recent elections, people have abandoned moderate forces and turned instead to the belligerent populisms of either the Right or the Left, characterized most of all by an emotionally powerful "us" and "them" campaigning zeal. On the right, this is the populism of Nigel Farage and Boris Johnson, grounded in the claim that the established elite disdain many ordinary people's cultural values, especially their scepticism about large-scale immigration and the apparent erosion of traditional British, or more accurately English, ways of life. On the left, the move has taken place largely within one of the established parties, Labour, but it is equally dependent on a core division. The conventional political elite, the argument goes here, have fallen into too cosy a relationship with the economic elite, leaving those suffering at the sharp end of Britain's unequal economy with nowhere to turn. The only course of action available is an aggressive, activist politics, one that scorns the conventions of Westminster, Whitehall, the City of London, the so-called mainstream media, and conservative opinion wherever it is to be found, and builds an argument for ideologically pure, systemic economic change to be created with the help of social movements mobilized through digital campaigns.[2]

I stepped away from this frenzy well before the pandemic. At that point, in 2017, and with much gut-wrenching self-doubt, I left my post as chief executive of one of Britain's largest and most left-leaning think tanks, the New Economics Foundation (NEF), for a return to academic life thousands of miles away with my wife, an Australian native returning to her homeland after decades away. In my time leading NEF, I had tried to convince its staff and its board to resist the siren songs of populism on either the left or the right. I believed that there had to be a way to heal Britain's political and social divides while still securing far-reaching economic reform. I just did not believe that those two goals were incompatible. It seemed, after all, that what most people were really looking for could be distilled in the aspiration to be given some kind of control of their own destiny again, rather than leaving everything in the hands of the elites of politics, the economy, or society. That is why the Brexiteers' slogan of "take back control" has proved so lastingly powerful. Beset by economic anxiety and political exclusion, people want their own lives reflected in their politics; their own values and experiences at the country's heart. In other words, the core of the argument remains from George Orwell, Priestley, and Dylan Thomas back in the 1930s and 1940s.

In 2016 and 2017, I made this case relentlessly at NEF, but the time was not right. We were living through the first blush of Corbynism, and riding on the back of Bernie Sanders's challenge for the Democratic Party nomination in the United States, at NEF, at least, belief in a Left populism was too strong. Class war in the name of systemic economic change was the name of the game there. In more conservative circles, meanwhile, people were digging into the Brexit trenches in the hope that leaving the EU would provide the control needed, and they were unwilling to look much beyond that. I had friends and allies in many corners of politics, journalism, philanthropy, and community life who were keen to help build an alternative case, but there was no major platform from which anyone could safely and effectively make the claim.

The case still needs to be made, though, and watching the last few years of British politics unfold from afar has strengthened rather than weakened that commitment. Populism offers no prospect of being able to restore calm to Britain's politics or to politics anywhere else in the world. Nor does it provide the means necessary actually to advance its own causes of change. The populism of the Right will not narrow the cultural divide between rulers and the ruled, as it promises. The gulf between Aaron Banks and the working people of Britain is just as vast as that which separates those people from Tony Blair. Nor will the populism of the Left truly build a new economy where the injustices of the past are swept away. Instead, it will leave the country more divided, more afflicted by bitterness and disdain, and potentially dealing with capital flight in the process. As Chantal Mouffe has it, that populism of the Left "sees the public sphere as the battlefield on which hegemonic projects confront one another with no possibility of a final reconciliation" and that determines the ways in which they work.[3] Populism of this kind is committed to the dominant role of power hierarchies in shaping political outcomes, enthusiastic about the place of raw emotions and negative passions in political argument, and determined to draw energy from dividing lines between those who are "in" and those who are "out." None of these are methods to restore the spirit of political possibility.

But the answer is not to return to the techniques of the era we have just left, as some so-called political moderates insist. The misleadingly easy prosperity of the 1990s is not coming back, nor is the kind of technocratic economic decision-making and distanced, professional political style that accompanied it. Indeed, many of the developments of that era—including the contracting out of public services to private corporations—have contributed to some of the worst crises of our own time. We need something else. We need a politics that acknowledges the need for deep, structural change but that rejects Manichean division; a politics that is committed to treating people with respect, no matter where they come from or what cultural aspirations they share, but that recognizes that there are important arguments to be had; a politics that realizes that wisdom does not reside in Whitehall, Westminster, or our leading universities alone, but seeks to find expertise in every corner of the country.

The answer lies in a politics of the everyday; a politics inspired by the ideas developed by Orwell, Priestley, Thomas, and their colleagues in an earlier age. Some may believe that this has never been possible, that politics and ordinary life just do not mix. Others might believe that it was an understandable approach for the twentieth century, but its time has passed. The task of this chapter is to change these doubters' minds. There is still genius to be found in the heart of Britain's communities, a genius that can drive the necessary change at the same time as it restores the long-lost calm to British political life. We just need to rediscover the imagination required to see it.

At the heart of the argument of this book is the celebration of the everyday. For all of their differences and disagreements, Bill Brandt, D. H. Lawrence, George Orwell, J. B. Priestley, Dylan Thomas, Barbara Jones, and the others we have followed here all agreed that there is something in life as it is usually lived by ordinary people that contains the source of great hope but that is missed by normal politics. Fulfilling, ordinary lives, they insisted, contain a sense of belonging to place, a feeling of community, a dedication to preserving the best of memory and past. Such life is small, not grand. Such lives grow in the parochial spaces and the familial. They are best described with texture and detail, not in the booming or the abstract. These lives too are enriched by an independence of spirit. They treasure the eccentricities and distinctiveness of people, the creativity and imagination and the peculiar patterns of custom and tradition that are displayed in different parts of the country. Politics is destructive and dangerous when it does not realize all of this. It can be inspiring and fulfilling—magical even—when it does.

This fundamental idea has never gone away, but like the other elements of British politics and culture, it has ebbed and flowed with the years. Recently, it has begun to surge to the surface once again, often in the most unlikely of places. To take just one powerful example, the British psychotherapist Adam Phillips has recently brilliantly developed his own version of the idea by describing the difference between what he calls "forbidden" and "unforbidden" pleasures.[4] Although the terminology might be unusual, Phillips's description of it is a profoundly helpful one. The forbidden pleasures, he says, are those that get all of the attention in public life. These are the boundary issues: the "what is permitted" and the "what is not permitted." In politics, that includes issues like sovereignty and nationhood, the constitutional rules governing elections and decision-making, and questions of economic control, social justice, systemic change, and the place of state and market in our lives. It is the realm, in other words, of bigness. Pursuing such pleasures emotionally provides a sense of importance and consequence, the feeling of dedicating one's life to a mighty cause, such as creating a better or fairer or greater world or preventing some grave evil. Rationally, it speaks to people's cognitive desire to create a blueprint for the future.

In contrast, what Phillips calls the "unforbidden pleasures" involve the bulk of what goes on every day. These are found in events like preparing and eating a regular family meal, meeting the kids at the school gate, having a chat with someone on the bus, walking in the park, checking in on an elderly friend or relative after work, going to the shops, planning a weekend away with friends. These pleasures matter to everyone enormously. They are the content of most of our lives, and most of us are pleased that they are. When we look through our memories, whether captured in photos, letters, or diaries or just at the backs of our minds, it is usually these unforbidden moments that loom the largest for all of us. They are the cause of the most intense enjoyment and sense of satisfaction. They reflect the connections and experiences that give meaning to our lives.

But despite all of this, they are hardly ever the business of politics as normally practiced. They don't appear on the news broadcasts or in the investigative journalists' reports. They are rarely the subject of the big policy arguments. They never feature on the cover page of an election manifesto. I was given a powerful reminder of this when I began working in formal politics back in 2010. I met with the Labour Party's pollster James Morris, who showed me reams and reams of opinion poll data on what it was that mattered most to the voters of Britain. The response at the top of every single survey was the wish to be able to have rewarding time with close friends and family. Nothing else came close. I asked James why Labour didn't do anything with this in its policy-making or its campaigning. Couldn't I write a speech about it? "It is just not the kind of thing that politics is about," came the confident reply.

There are times, of course, when individual elements within these two categories switch between them. When governments attempt to prohibit everyday acts that had previously been taken for granted, then the unforbidden can become the forbidden. This was precisely the cause of Orwell's deepest terror in *Nineteen Eighty-Four*. What would society be like, he asked, if basic, unremarkable, entirely everyday pleasures, such as beginning a romance, telling stories to your children, buying a present for a friend, were suddenly prohibited by the government, with your every effort to engage in them monitored and repressed? How intensely would we suffer? How could we plausibly resist? Likewise, there are also occasionally moments when the reverse occurs, when previously deeply controversial practices cease to be controversial and forbidden pleasures becomes unforbidden one. Changing attitudes and legislative practices might be enabling gay and lesbian relationships to move towards being an example of this kind in many places across the world right now, with a once strictly forbidden pleasure now entering the realm of the unforbidden.

Even if the precise content of the categories can change over time, though, Phillips insists that the distinction itself remains crucial. And that is because when it comes to politics, almost all of the energy and time tends to be sucked up with an argument about the forbidden—often understood as the big—and overlooks the unforbidden, often dubbed the small. And this is not without consequences. When human beings spend their time thinking about the forbidden—what should and should not be permitted in society—they can become harsher, more determined, more narrow-minded people, more likely to see the world in "us" and "them," even "friend" and "enemy," than when their attention is on the unforbidden.

Even if this focus does not result in hostility and conflict, thinking on the forbidden has a tendency to draw attention like a magnet, depriving people of the emotional and cognitive space to attend to other, more mundane elements of their lives. "When it comes to the forbidden," Phillips writes, "we are not supposed to let our minds wander; we are supposed to be utterly gripped, and in the grip of the law."[5] The result is both that people's lives are impoverished—they are drawn away from everyday fulfilments that are just there waiting to be achieved—and, paradoxically, that they are not even able to function effectively in the realm of the forbidden, emotionally exhausted as they are from the constant pressure to be "on top" of what confronts them with no sustaining internal resource on which to draw.

Phillips, then, longs for an alternative. He wants people to find far greater space in their lives, including in their political lives, for the unforbidden pleasures. He wants us to step back from the immediacy and urgency of the so-called big arguments and to take time to revel in and experiment with the small and otherwise unremarkable aspects of our life. "Promoting unforbidden pleasures means finding new kinds of heroes and heroines (or dispensing with them altogether)," he says, and it "privileges the more ordinary at the cost of whatever we take to be the alternatives to the ordinary."[6] For Phillips, this begins with the power of everyday relationships. We should "start with the simple acknowledgement that it is extraordinary how much pleasure we can get from each other's company, most of which is unforbidden," he says.[7] Ordinary family and friendship, neighbourliness and collegiality, are thus at the heart of Phillips's vision of a life lived with the unforbidden as a focal point. It is a small step from there to the same bundle of concerns that were the essence of Orwell's, Priestley's, and Thomas's ideal, including the importance of an everyday sense of belonging to place, a feeling of community with one's fellows, and a continuity with the ordinary memories of the past.

The idea of the unforbidden also causes us to look again at our own place in the unfolding of history. Those who think mostly on the forbidden, rather than the unforbidden, often do so because they believe those are the things that really matter, they are the factors that will determine the lives we can all live in the future. Dwelling in the ordinary and the everyday, the small rather than the big, can deprive us of a sense that we can be a personal agent of great change. Some of us, especially those of us drawn to politics, can find that an enormous psychological challenge. How can we give up the sense that we are directly, personally responsible—at least in part—for the creation of a better future? The answer lies in an ability to extend what we are able to do, think, and feel in the present, as opposed to in the future. Seeing the world through the lens of the unforbidden places the present far closer to the centre of our concern. As the American sociologist Andrew Abbott puts it, seen this way, the challenge for our lives ceases to be how each of us can play a part in improving an imaginary future state and instead becomes how we can learn to avail ourselves of every means necessary to extend our experience in the now and the repeated nows to come.[8]

Abbott does not mean this in a selfish or individualistic way. This is not a call for narrow-minded hedonism. Instead, he wishes us to develop an ability to enrich both our experience and the experience of others in the here and now. And he believes that we best do that by cultivating a tenderness and curiosity that can expand our sense of the world and people around us. If, he explains, we cultivate "the habit of looking for new meanings, of seeking out new connections, of investing experience with complexity or extension," then we can make that experience feel both "richer and longer, even though it remains anchored in some local bit of both social space and social time."[9]

Nor does a focus on the unforbidden mean we cease to consider the importance of the future at all. Of course not. Rather, it means letting go of the hubristic idea that our personal role in developing our most desired future outcome determines the likelihood of that outcome and thus our future pleasures and the pleasures of others. Such a view overstates our own personal importance, the likelihood of our success and the chance that even if we got where we wanted, it would prove as worthwhile as we think. Moreover, by using the very idea of an "outcome," it presumes that there is some moment in the future that is more important than the present, when everything will somehow stop. But that is clearly false. Even the future will be the present once we actually arrive at it. There are no outcomes in human lives beyond death. Our task, then, at least in part, must be to know how to experience something meaningful and worthwhile in that "future present," both for ourselves and for those around us, whether or not that future looks or feels as we hoped that it might.

On the surface, this talk of the unforbidden can look suspiciously like an abandonment of all that is conventionally held to be important in public life. Its celebration of smallness can look like a rejection of bigness. It can seem conservative, rather than radical, committed to seeing change, at worst, as something to be regretted or, at best, as something that is shaped only by forces larger than ourselves. It can also seem woefully smug. It is all too easy, after all, for those who do reasonably well in the present social, economic, and political order to tell everyone else to sit back and enjoy the moment, rather than to join a struggle for change.

These selfsame charges were, of course, laid directly at Orwell's, Priestley's, and Thomas's doors at the very beginning of the Second World War. Their apparent desire to avoid the fight, to warn their compatriots off getting too emotionally involved in foreign affairs, and to encourage them to concentrate on the immediate, the here and now, was often condemned as a kind of political "quietism." How was it morally acceptable just to sit back at a time like that? Similar charges were laid during the postwar period. As the Attlee government got on with the job of securing full employment, nationalizing industries, and creating a welfare state, critics thought that Orwell, Thomas, and Priestley were just carping from the sidelines. The fact that there was no meaningful political resistance in *Nineteen Eighty-Four* or any explicit politics in *Under Milk Wood* did not go unnoticed.

Thomas was unmoved by these criticisms. They were rooted, he insisted, in an unconvincing belief in the necessity of either/or choices. But it didn't need to be like that. Surely, he thought, the big and the small, the grand and the everyday, the forbidden and the unforbidden could live together. People can exist with elements of each, existing in the tension, if you like, and politics could also address itself to both in turn. Thomas made this claim in his own wonderfully evocative style when he wrote in 1938 to his politically active friend Henry Teece. Teece had despaired of Thomas's insistence on writing poetry about the everyday occurrences of a small rural village instead of about the grand political challenges of the day. Thomas replied,

> You are right when you suggest I think a squirrel stumbling at least of equal importance to Hitler's invasions, murder in Spain, the Garbo-Stokowski romance, royalty, Horlicks, lynchlaw, pit disaster, Joe Louis, wicked capitalists, saintly communists, democracy, the Ashes, the Church of England, birth control, Yeats' voice, the machines of the world I tick and revolve in, pub-baby-weather-government-football-youthandage-speed-lipstick, all small tyrannies, means tests, the fascist anger, the daily, momentary lightings, eruptions, farts, dampsquibs, barrel-organs, tinwhistles, howitzers, tiny death-rattles, volcanic whimpers of the world I eat, drink, love, work hard and delight in—but I am aware of these things as well.[10]

The idea that these two modes could be meaningfully combined has two dimensions. First, there is the notion that politics can be conducted in a way that does not undermine the crucial features of the everyday but instead protects and enhances them, fostering qualities like friendship, care, and a sense of belonging to community and place that are themselves only immediately discovered in more ordinary, everyday settings. Second, there is the suggestion that political action itself might somehow begin in the everyday—in the realm of the unforbidden—and then move to the more conventional realm and that it might actually become stronger and more effective on its own terms as a result. This is the notion at the heart of the community organizing practised by groups like Citizens UK, which prioritizes the building of connections between citizens in everyday settings to the taking of immediate political action like electoral campaigning, but which nonetheless also seek standard political outcomes, including changes in legislation, in the longer run. Relationship precedes action, the community-organizing mantra goes, it does not replace action. And that is as good a summary as any of the overall argument.[11]

Both of these possibilities require significant changes to the ways in which politics is currently conducted. At the moment, those who are closest to official politics are often openly contemptuous of the everyday and the unforbidden. For decades now, the professionalization of political parties and the bureaucratization of government have generated a cult of expertise and detachment, a sense that ordinary people do not understand their own lives, that the fundamental aspects of their affairs are better run for them from on high either by the officials of the state or by the giants of the market. In this vein, ordinary people's absorption in the everyday pleasures of life—be it family, television, holidays, hobbies, or the past—is often taken as a sign that they have got their priorities wrong and that they cannot be trusted to make the decisions that really matter.

But this is not just a problem of formal or official politics. Contemporary activist politics is not much better in this regard. In fact, it is sometimes worse. The desire for ideological purity that is characteristic of many campaigning groups frequently leads them to denounce a host of everyday activities as, at best, irrelevant to the larger struggle or, at worst, a contribution to the very injustices that should be fought. When I was at NEF, for example, the most ideologically committed regularly hosted all-staff meetings that they called "living our values." Despite the uplifting name, these gatherings disguised a community that could be spectacularly intolerant of those among them who continued to live their lives in a host of other very ordinary ways, such as buying their lunch at one of the major supermarkets or drinking from the occasional plastic bottle of water. The unforbidden was morphed into the forbidden. Such practices will be well known to anyone who has spent time in an activist community in the last five years; they are precisely what makes so many ordinary people so hostile to the woke.

If anyone is to have any hope of restoring trust in politics, all of this has to stop. The cynicism and contempt for people at its core are just too transparent. As the socialist literary critic Raymond Williams once argued, to find resonance in the world, political activists have to avoid making "the extraordinary error of believing that most people only become interesting when they begin to engage with political . . . actions of a previously recognized kind." Instead, "if we are serious about even political life, we have to enter that world in which people live as they can as themselves . . . within a whole complex of work and love and illness and natural beauty."[12]

This point is so simple, and it has been laboured by political consultants, leadership strategists, and speechwriters for years now, and yet it appears overwhelmingly difficult for politicians to grasp. Of course, populist demagogues try to some degree to close the gap in style between the political elite and the everyday. Britain has become used to seeing Nigel Farage with his cigar and his pint or Boris Johnson and his floppy hair and ruffled shirt. And the basic lesson has been heard even by the mainstream. Almost every candidate for prime minister now tries at some point to share a personal narrative, a story about themselves grounded in childhood and community. When I was a political speechwriter, the primary task was always to encourage politicians to discuss their origins, their personal mission, and the important personal moments in their lives, and we drew on some wonderful literary and theatrical talents to try to do so. But despite all of the advice and all of the good intentions, nothing of any significance in the style of our politics has really changed. There has been no serious politician in Britain in recent years capable of speaking effectively about the everyday, let alone capable of reflecting a deep concern with the rhythms of actual people's ordinary lives. If anything, the hostility and intense disruption of the last few years have pushed politicians further and further the other way.

The change needed is not just about political style, of course. It is also about content. For all of its frustrations, politics matters, because whether we like it or not, it permits some kinds of actions and prohibits others. Even the most ardent adherent to the idea of unforbidden pleasures has to acknowledge that legislation and regulation shape practical possibilities. If we really care about a politics of the everyday, it is vital for the content of such legislation and regulation to be beneficial to the development of unforbidden pleasures, rather than a hindrance. We need a public policy programme underpinned by a concern for the everyday.

Perhaps the fullest recent effort to identify the outline of such a programme has come from the world-leading public health researcher and former director of maternal and infant health at the World Health Organization, Anthony Costello, in his superb book, *The Social Edge*. Written shortly before he shot to prominence as one of the leading critics of the Johnson government's response to COVID-19, Costello's central question is a simple one: What kind of public policies might enable people to develop reliable and emotionally sustaining relationships with each other in small, everyday settings? His conclusion is that this requires people to be members of what he calls "sympathy groups," small, informal, but relatively predictable gatherings of people who come together in ways that require little in the way of official, bureaucratic oversight. This can include groups such as those that already exist "for sport, choirs, prayer, books, farming, service quality, investment, gardening, yoga, cards, childcare, audit, fraternity and sorority," and even, in some contexts, "recreational drug use like qat-chewing, drinking beer, hookah pipes, and wine-tasting." The multiple advantages of these groups, Costello tells us, have little to do with their specific purpose; rather, they emerge incidentally from the fact that they "provide us with time to interact with our friends, neighbours and club members," which in turn generates "more happiness and a greater sense of being alive."[13] They are stronger when they draw in a diverse range of participants, enabling people not just to bond with those whom they already know but also to bridge to those whose experiences have not been the same as their own. Their flourishing is also, Costello contends, a proxy for a more general sense of the psychological health of people's everyday lives.

As a scientist, Costello argues that the best way to discover the kind of public policies required to assist the development of these groups is by persuading the government to initiate a series of policy experiments and, if possible, randomized controlled trials. The whole gamut of recent public policy clearly presents a reasonable field for such work. Anyone concerned with promoting everyday relationships will agree that we should test action to prevent the increasing social segregation of communities along lines of class and wealth, to halt the shrinking of open-to-access public space, to slow the increase in the number of people unable to spend time with families and friends because of the demands of paid work, and to release people from the burdens of cutthroat competition in the workplace. Unsurprisingly, then, the list of Costello's proposals for experiments is gigantic, ranging from measuring the effect of relatively small endeavours such as empowering voluntary groups in the provision of health and social services to much more demanding efforts such as creating large community-led cooperatives in vital areas of the economy.

We would no doubt learn enormously from Costello's experiments, and we should try to conduct them or at least to encourage others to do so. But we also do not need to wait for the evidence to come in. For we know who the real experts in everyday relationships and unforbidden pleasures are already. And that is ordinary people themselves. The central reason why we have a politics that is so stuck in the grand and the abstract is that we have a politics that prioritizes centralized decision-making and elite guidance over real and genuine popular control. The partisanship of Westminster and the technical expertise of Whitehall, vital though both are, are never likely to generate a politics that is sensitive and sympathetic to the power of the everyday. Britain's failures when the pandemic first reached its shores are clear proof of that. What that means most of all is that Britain requires a thoroughgoing devolution of power.

That devolution could begin almost anywhere. The big, formal institutions of government naturally present the greatest target. Brexit might provide an ideal moment to share power far beyond London to the cities and regions, as well as more fully still with the constituent nations of the United Kingdom. The local authorities of Britain have huge official responsibilities for local services, including care for the elderly and the education of children, but they have astonishingly little power actually to shape those services, let alone to raise revenue to enable them to do so. They are penned in on all sides by commands from London, and almost all of their income is dependent on the whim of the central government. Enormous energies could be released simply by freeing these authorities from those diktats, even in a select number of areas. This is no doubt true in other political systems and traditions too. For even where local authorities are more formally empowered—such as in the United States and parts of Europe—there remains a powerful informal sense that elites should drive the decisions that really matter to people's lives.

The division between politics and the everyday that so many people now take for granted could, therefore, begin to be healed if there was a real possibility of allowing local knowledge to influence the provision of local services or of enabling local people to actively play a part in shaping local economies. Such large-scale institutional change might, of course, prove too hard in the short term. Change could, however, still begin almost immediately within a range of other public services and the workplace. There are multiple opportunities for popular engagement and the sharing of real control in large-scale organizations that fall outside the direct control of government, some of which are increasingly being grasped already. In National Health Service hospitals, power can be shared with patient groups and their families; in universities, with students, their parents, and neighbouring communities; in businesses, with workers, customers, and neighbours;

in social housing estates, with residents, potential residents, and even former residents. The precise details are, of course, extraordinarily complex to work out in each case, but the general principle is just as strikingly straightforward. If we want decision-making to better reflect the cares, concerns, and rhythms of ordinary life, then ordinary people should be directly engaged in making and implementing them.

Nor, if we are serious, should such power sharing stop at this level. Campaign groups, activist networks, and local political parties could also take a lead. As explained earlier, too frequently at the moment, these groups mimic the exclusionary, aggressive, "us and them" mindset of the organs of formal politics, and they close the door on the everyday, the unforbidden, as they do so. But it does not need to be like that. If even a handful of campaigning groups made a genuine commitment to working with the grain of the everyday rather than against it, if they made conscious efforts not endlessly to criticize and condemn the ordinary lives of ordinary people, then positive change would result. This would not mean such groups taking a vow of silence on everyday practices that they find deeply challenging, of course. No one is suggesting that antiracism groups should fail to respond to everyday racism or gender equality groups should reserve judgement in the face of everyday sexism. Nor should it mean groups shy away from controversy, from picking a fight where fights are needed or from laying out arguments that radically break from the status quo. But it should mean that when groups do these things, they interrogate themselves in each instance and resist defaulting to destructive hubris and aggression simply because it is the standard mode of the conventionally political.

This is an agenda of real reform derived from the belief that there is untapped strength in the everyday. It is an agenda that shows how each of the style, policy content, institutions, and campaigning that makes up our political lives may be adapted better to reflect the importance of the unforbidden pleasures in the rest of our lives. More important still, it is happening already.

I discovered this personally in 2015. Having lost the general election with Ed Miliband and suddenly finding myself without a sense of purpose, I was looking for a space in which to write, our Hackney flat being both too small and too noisy. My wife spotted a notice in a local coffee shop offering the share of half a desk in the basement of the Round Chapel, a beautiful but slightly run down nineteenth-century church on the Lower Clapton Road, minutes from where we lived. I paid the deposit and began heading to the basement daily for work. There were four others using the basement, one of whom was a photographer, Jørn Tomter, who took overall responsibility for the space. It was initially a bit depressing. I had, after all, moved from an office in the Palace of Westminster to a windowless basement in Hackney. Little did I know that I was about to receive a political lesson as important as anything that I had learnt fighting elections.

Talking with Jørn, I realized something that I hadn't thought about half enough in all of my years in professional politics. There was a small group of people trying to turn strained communities into wonderful, fulfilling, and exciting places to live, not by lobbying for large-scale legislation or by campaigning for political parties but by acting immediately in the heart of the everyday. Jørn had set up a tiny organization, I Love Chatsworth Road, named after the quirky, socially diverse shopping street just round the corner, to try to cultivate a sense of wonder in a neighbourhood regularly portrayed in the national press as blighted by poverty, crime, and ethnic and religious tension. He went into local schools to take photos of the kids so that every family could have a portrait whether they had the money or not. He produced a local newspaper where local people told stories of the neighbourhood's past and shared their plans for the present. And he got people together at night in the cafés, to give them a chance to run social events that they could design themselves. It was beautiful.[14]

Chatsworth Treecircle
© Jørn Tomter

And it was efforts like these that helped the neighbourhood through the most difficult days of COVID-19 too.

This kind of effort is, of course, now far more wide-ranging than Jørn in his basement. Right across Britain, the last few years have witnessed an explosion in practical efforts to work in just this way. One of the largest of these efforts is the Every One, Every Day initiative run by the Participatory City Foundation, masterminded by the social entrepreneur Tessy Britton, in the East London Borough of Barking and Dagenham. Founded on the idea that "what people do together every day matters," Every One, Every Day fosters and facilitates "widespread networks of co-operation and friendship" in one of the most economically deprived and ethnically diverse communities in the whole of the UK. It does so in a host of projects, each and every one of which is codesigned and coproduced by ordinary residents themselves.

In its first year alone, funded by both the local council and a host of major philanthropic foundations, Every One, Every Day has seen at least two thousand people involved in forty different ongoing projects, including taking over shops on the high street and turning them into welcoming spaces for people to meet and socialize, cultivating disused public land as community gardens where people can grow food to eat, providing spaces and equipment for families from different backgrounds to cook together and to entertain their children, and opening a warehouse equipped with free-to-use tools, IT equipment, sewing machines, laser cutters, coworking space, financial advice, and a cooperatively run childcare facility to help foster new community businesses.[15] The ambition is enormous. "This is hope at last," one participant told the *Guardian*'s reporter George Monbiot when he visited. "Hope for my generation. Hope for my grandchildren."[16]

That hope doesn't just lie with Every One, Every Day. There is a similar initiative in Wigan, in the north of England, where the local council has worked to create the Deal, which it describes as an "informal agreement between the council and everyone who lives or works here to work together to create a better borough." Deal projects include programmes for supporting community businesses, for enabling children and young people to exercise their own influence in shaping education and social services, and a wholly new way of providing social care to the elderly, developed on the principle that residents should never be approached as "a collection of needs and problems" but rather as "unique individuals, who have strengths, assets, gifts and talents." The same principle motivates the "People in the Lead" strategy adopted in 2015 by the Big Lottery Foundation, the largest community grant-giving foundation in the UK. "We want to start with what people bring to the table, not what they don't have; and from the belief that people and communities are best placed to solve their problems, take advantage of opportunities, and rise to challenges," the Big Lottery's CEO, Dawn Austwick, insists. "From this everything else follows." Similar declarations have followed from other multimillion-pound philanthropic trusts and foundations, including the Paul Hamlyn Foundation and the Esmee Fairbairn Foundation, as well as from think tanks and pressure groups, including Participle, whose founder, Hilary Cottam, has literally written the textbook on this new approach in her masterful *Radical Help*, and the New Local Government Network, whose new "community paradigm" is a long list of practical instructions to local authorities and service providers that has at its core just "one shared feature: handing power over to communities."[17]

This is wonderful and profoundly important work, connecting elements of the everyday to the deep business of social change in a way that echoes the fundamental goals of the Festival of Britain for a new time. It is too early to evaluate the impact of each individual effort fully, of course. That will come sure enough. But it offers a new sense of direction. Despite all of this, it still goes almost wholly unnoticed in the world of mainstream politics. No current political leader speaks of it. No one includes it in their manifestos. Perhaps they are put off by the unwarranted sense that it is too close to David Cameron's ill-fated Big Society, a much less forthright ambition.

This absence of interest also extends to those whose job it is to explain politics to the public. As the conservatively inclined *New York Times* columnist David Brooks has explained, professional journalists "barely cover" the efforts of these "social change agents" because they are dismissed as "goody-goody." But, he continues, "these people are not goody-goody. They are raw, honest and sometimes rude. How do we in our business get in that spot where we spend 90 percent of our coverage on the 10 percent of our lives influenced by politics and 10 percent of our coverage on the 90 percent of our lives influenced by relationship, community and the places we live every day?"[18] The explanation lies, as Adam Phillips tells us, in our inability to take our eyes off the forbidden, when we should be looking at the potential of the unforbidden. Brooks gets things a bit wrong, though. For this kind of grounded changemaking, with its roots firmly planted in community and the everyday, is not best seen as an *alternative* to politics. It should, instead, be understood as a new kind of politics. Not only that, it is the biggest source of hope in a profoundly dark time.

Hope it might be. But what if it is too little and what if it is too late? What if the times are too dark for whatever light this kind of politics might bring? There is no doubt that we live in an era of enormous democratic disruption, a time when populist forces are ripping through the orthodox institutions, calling ad nauseum for the abolition of the BBC, the destruction of centuries-old legal conventions, and the abolition of crucial human rights. It is a time of deepening climate emergency, spiralling economic inequality, and rapid and disorientating technological change; a time when millions of young British people believe that they face a future without affordable housing, stable employment, or a secure safety net from the welfare state. And it is a time when politics seems incapable of responding. It is a moment of Twitter wars and dark social media arts, of fake news on Facebook, of deep distrust of the new and the unseen, alongside rampant foreign interference in national democratic practices.

In an age like this, the demand that politics embrace the mundane and the parochial, the ordinary and the everyday, can seem puny at best and indulgent at worst. Shouldn't we be trying, as my old boss Ed Miliband has argued, to get the whole nation on a "war footing" in response to these ills? Or, as Greta Thunberg even more evocatively suggests, isn't the best response just to panic?[19]

Such responses are wholly understandable—we live in frightening times—but they also miss the point. For the quest to overcome our current ills and the effort to draw politics and the everyday together are intricately related. And the relationship has deep roots. Our current age of despair is the direct consequence of the rupture of politics from everyday life. If political parties, public service providers, and campaigners had attended more to the unforbidden pleasures and ordinary rhythms of life in the last few decades, then trust in our institutions would be higher, our nation would be less unequal, and our communities would cohere more strongly. We're falling apart precisely because we have failed to try. It may well turn out that it is too late for this generation to change that after all—that's what the concluding chapter will explore—but it is certainly our duty to try.

CONCLUSION

The Magic of Everyday Life

A FEW YEARS AGO, I was walking in London's Lincoln's Inn Fields, a beautiful, expansive, historic square just near the London School of Economics, meeting a friend. It was dusk, a London summer's evening just setting in, the light was changing, and on the north side of the square the crowds were lining for a nighttime opening of the quirky old museum known as Sir John Soane's. It was still and quiet, apart from the occasional excited chatter of the museumgoers echoing around the square. The pavements there are wide, so I was strolling happily, arms swinging, without any fear of being knocked down by a car. I had done a day's work and was looking forward to the evening. And then for a moment, just as my friend cycled up, everything stood still. I can remember the crispness of the moment intensely. Entirely ordinary, but entirely magical at the same time. If I close my eyes right now, here thousands of miles away, I can be back there still.

In her wonderful book *Ordinary Affects*, the anthropologist Kathleen Stewart both chronicles and analyses experiences just such as these. She calls them "still life." A still life, she tells us, is a "simple stopping." It is a moment in ordinary life when time seems to come to a halt; a moment when the mundane turns into "a dreaming scene, if only for a minute." As we stand within those moments, our mind can race, shooting with ideas about what really matters in the world, discovering sudden insights, even epiphanies. Alternatively, it can pause, finding restorative repose from the helter-skelter concerns of work or politics and becoming absorbed in some unforbidden pleasure, perhaps one that we've never even noticed we cared about as much before.[1] We don't leave the ordinary world at these times. We are profoundly situated, placed, rooted. But we exist in that world in a different way from normal. Even if for just a second, we draw insight, strength, connection, a sense of humane depth from the everyday.[2]

These moments are at the heart of the art and literature discussed in this book. D. H. Lawrence was in a still life when he finally felt at home in the world watching the mowers with their scythes "*slush! slush!*" through the grass in "Insouciance." George Orwell had George Bowling find the same peace staring into the pond in *Coming Up for Air*, watching "the Newts, water-snails, water-beetles, caddis-flies, leeches" just for seconds but wishing it could last "ten lifetimes."[3] Dylan Thomas encouraged us all to try to share such a moment when he had the narrator at the very outset of *Under Milk Wood* beckon us to hush as we listen to the "sloeblack, slow, black, crowblack, fishingboatbobbing sea."[4] Barbara Jones was thrilled to find canal-boat craftsmen enjoy these same moments, escaping the "ever more fretful life" by spending their time sunk in the process of creation.[5]

Given the difference to the frenzied speed and sharp contrasts of contemporary politics, this evocation of moments of stillness in the everyday can seem a world away. As the philosopher Sheldon Wolin told us, within our current political life, the "mind is not given much to reflection or contemplation and does not easily give itself over to mental rhythms suggestive of calm and serenity."[6] But out of these moments of calmness, out of these reflections on the ordinary world around us, can come the most profound political lessons. It was recollecting moments like this that led Thomas to describe the value of community in terms of the shared memories of everyday life, whether it be childhood trips to the beach or roving through the suburban streets at night in search of a good night out. It was capturing them on film that enabled Bill Brandt to shape a conception of nationhood that helped shepherd Britain through the Second World War. And it was the anxiety that they would be monitored and repressed that terrified Orwell into writing *Nineteen Eighty-Four*.

The task facing our own age, then, is truly to attend to these very ordinary but very powerful moments once again, and to see what we can learn from them for our own political times. That involves, in part, fighting for the kinds of public policies that make moments like these more frequent and more fulfilling. We have a good sense of what that involves, even before we have conducted the kinds of experiments that Anthony Costello called us to in Chapter 7. As the British historian Jon Lawrence and the American sociologist Eric Klinenberg have both separately shown, it requires us to build real "social infrastructure."[7] That means publicly provided, free-to-use spaces for people to meet and socialize safely and without fear, even after pandemic. It means easy access to the beauty of the natural environment, be it in the form of urban parks or the expanses of the countryside. It means schools that teach people not only how to pass exams but also how to live well together. It means too doing what we can to reform as many workplaces as possible, so they are not alienating and hierarchical experiences that suck the life and soul out of us, but where we feel we can share a sense of purpose with others and learn and develop new ways of looking at the world, as well as making ends meet. This requires no less than the building of what the American political thinker Danielle Allen calls a "connected society."[8] It is an agenda of enormous change. And all of it, as I also argued in Chapter 7, is more likely to come about when actual power is shared and when the voices of everyday people play a larger role than ever in shaping the circumstances of their everyday lives.

It also means campaigning for all of these changes in a different way. Concern for the everyday can, and should, be a constraint on the ways in which we conduct ourselves in politics. It should haul us back from taking refuge in the language of the grand and the abstract. It should discourage us from the mechanical thinking of the techno-crat, uninterested in the ways in which our recommendations play out and are experienced in the actual lives of actual people. It should prevent us from the aggressive, polarizing, "us and them" spirit of the populists, whether of the Right or the Left. But it is not just a con-straint; it is an opportunity too. For if we were to find a way to relate our political campaigning more effectively to the experience of the everyday—even if only particular aspects or moments within the everyday—then we would have a chance of reconnecting millions of people to the political process who are currently tired and dispirited by what they have seen of it for years now. This is not just a matter of convincing people that politics matters to the shape of their lives. Most people see that already. It is a matter of persuading them that politics can be run by them and run in their own image.

Some will no doubt mock all of this as nostalgia. If there ever was a time for the politics of the everyday, it has now passed. They will say that protecting ourselves from virus requires us all to spend less time with each other and not more; or that the robots are coming and now is not the time to distract ourselves with sentiment; or the climate is heating up too quickly to be worried about identity; or in-equality is too sharp for us ever to imagine people coming together across social divides. Critics will also insist that social hatreds are too intense for the kind of communitarian politics this vision implies. Britain is breaking up. The union might soon be done for. Even if it holds on, societies are too divided now, the charge will come. Britain is now a far more multicultural society than it was in the immediate postwar years. It is alert to the need to acknowledge and recognize difference. As such, most people are rightly unwilling to endure the exclusionary social conservatism that often underpinned the community life of years gone by. Those who hanker for a return to this past, it is suggested, are often just hankering for the dominance of one social group—heterosexual, cisgender white men, in particular—over other social groups. And that is a decidedly unattractive basis on which to try to build a new political order.

Widespread though this argument is, it is also ultimately unconvincing. Of course, there are those who invoke the past in order to advance undesirable supremacist agendas. And we need to call them out. But the advantage of drawing on the everyday as the basis of our shared identity rather than on some purer, grander notion of race or nation or history or language is precisely that it can bind people together in shared experiences independent of their background. That is what Thomas looked for in Swansea growing up and in Laugharne as an adult; the children of rich and poor, of Tories and socialists, of English speakers and Welsh, of Church in Wales believers and nonconformists, creating a life together in the suburban streets, the parks, the pubs, and the snooker halls.

There is no doubt in my mind that much of that still exists, or at least can. It is the essence of the vision that animates groups like the wonderful youth-led migrants' rights campaigners We Belong. Created by young people who have endured the perils of irregular migration status in the UK, We Belong explains that formal citizenship status is of far less moral importance than the sense that someone has grown up with us as a fellow school student, a neighbour, a colleague, or a friend. Seen this way, the rights of migrants and refugees are derived not from any abstract ideal but from the fact that we share a life together. It is that fact that provides both the rights' moral core and the practical means of their recognition.

Spend the afternoon sitting in the launderette on the Lower Clapton Road, in Clapton, East London, and you will see what they

Chatsworth
© Jørn Tomter

mean. There you will see people who have come to London from all over the world and those who have been born a hundred metres away, religious and nonreligious, disabled and nondisabled, in paid work and not in paid work, citizen and noncitizen, talking and recognizing each other, with reference not to anything grand but only to the everyday. The ties that bind in Clapton come from conversations about COVID-19, childcare, buses, the new supermarket down the road, and even, now and again, the washing itself. They decidedly don't come from passports or grand cultures or narrow nationalisms. Of course, there is still racism to be fought and intolerance to be challenged. And on a bad day the launderette is full of both. But the everyday can be marshalled for the cause of right in that struggle, not only the cause of wrong.

There is nonetheless a version of this argument that is more com-pelling: the suggestion that the building blocks of the everyday itself are at risk. Seen this way, two new phenomena are undermining our shared experience of ordinary life: digital technologies and an austerity-driven erosion of the public sphere. Taken together, these two forces are increasingly *personalizing* our moments of satisfaction, our unforbidden pleasures. Absorbed in our screens and locked in our bedrooms, we are no longer sharing in public events in the same way that we used to. We are not sitting in pubs, we are playing with our iPads; we are not hanging out with our neighbours in the park, we are photographing our food and uploading it to "friends" we never see and may not ever have met on Instagram. A shared politics cannot be built out of such diverse and disparate materials, the argument goes. There is no twenty-first-century equivalent of a shared everyday in the way that there was in the twentieth, and thus this whole mission is misconceived.

There is much that is true in this concern. The infrastructure that facilitates shared experiences was weakening before the pandemic and now is more weakened still. The general experience of the English seaside, the urban park, the suburban pub, or the secluded rural vil-lage on which Thomas depended for his short stories is clearly far less widely shared now. Orwell would struggle to write a *Lion and the Uni-corn* today. People don't cluster around their television sets or radios as a community anymore, dissecting the same shows and revelling in the shared experience. They don't even watch the same programmes at home and discuss them at work or in the playground as they did in the later twentieth century. The filter bubbles of social media erode the sense of togetherness still further. Goodness knows what would happen if the BBC were actually to disappear, as the partisans on both sides of politics now demand.

Moreover, the mutual hatred of Brexit tribes may well drive people apart for years to come. Westminster politics offers precious little sign of being a space for unification. There certainly could be no meaningful twenty-first-century official, government-sponsored Festival of Britain. Immersed as we now are in culture wars over the history of empire, we can no longer agree about the fundamental story of Britain's past, let alone about its future. That is why when Theresa May suggested organizing a new festival to mark the seventieth anniversary of Gerald Barry and Hugh Casson's, she was widely and mercilessly mocked.

For all of the justified gloom, this erosion, however, makes the task of remembering the earlier age more important rather than less. In trying to think of a better future, that is, the resources of the past can act as a powerful rebuke to the tendencies of the present. As Bonnie Honig puts it, even looking upon a ruin "may yet point to a different future" because it reminds us that different possibilities exist to otherwise apparently unavoidable tendencies of the present. Zadie Smith has made the same point. "Apocalyptic scenarios" do not help, she says. Rather the "only thing that [can] create the necessary traction in our minds [is] the intimate loss of the things we love."[9] Seen this way, even in moments of utter devastation, the evocation of the richness of the past can "help to furnish an empty world."[10] We witnessed that, after all, in these very pages, when we saw Dylan Thomas grasping for his memories of a stronger, more collective time as he was mired in the depths of his own personal depression as the Second World War took hold. For Thomas at that time, it was only the properties of his memory that remained.

Before we reach for this consolation, though, it is also worth recognizing that we have not reached the point of desperation quite yet. Our times are not yet as bad as the outbreak of the war. If the critics actually attended a little more to the British everyday rather than to the shambles of parliamentary politics or the shrillest of the tweets, then they would see that much life in Britain is still very much shared, despite all of the inequalities and the tensions. Almost everything that continues to grab the attention of millions on British television, for example, is grounded in a distinct, parochial, unmistakably local story. For all of the worries about it falling apart, Britain is a country still telling a story about itself, and that story differs from place to place. All this was clear during the early days of the pandemic, from the "clap for carers" to PE with Joe Wicks. Beyond that, comedy is probably the most telling space. From Peter Kay's *Car Share* to Phoebe Waller-Bridge's *Fleabag*, from Steve Coogan's *Alan Partridge* to Reece Shearsmith and Steve Pemberton's *Inside No. 9*, these are stories that their writers know will resonate precisely because, for all their absurdity, they are still shared. In all of them, the spirit of Bill Brandt is alive and well. The same is true of the decisions that giant corporations make as they advertise their wares. There is nothing more ordinarily, if ironically, British than the standard television advert for a global chain like McDonald's in the UK. On a good day, the concept notes could have originated from a reading of *Portrait of the Artist as a Young Dog*. This is corporate co-optation, of course, and it is dangerous. It would have angered Hugh Casson and Barbara Jones beyond words. But it shows the power of the fundamental idea nonetheless.

For now, then, there is still much to work with, much to protect, and much to take strength from. When my dad, borrowing from Brandt, Orwell, Priestley, Thomas, and others, settled me down with stories of Britain in the Blitz all those years ago, he seeded in my head and my heart a spirit of hope. It was a hope grounded in the belief that ordinary people living everyday lives can achieve extraordinary things, for themselves, their communities, the nation, and the world. That hope is still very much alive. We know the truth of it from our own lives. We continue to see glimpses of it all the time. The task now is to turn it once again from a general sense of aspiration, a faith in one's fellow citizens, to a political project and even a governing programme. As we have seen, that will not be easy. It requires a struggle against so many of the conventions of politics, enabling us to see the merits of the small and not just the big, the parochial as well as the global, the concrete as well as the abstract, the past as well as the future. Given the state of Britain and the state of the world, there is urgency to this effort. COVID-19, Brexit, the undermining of the union, climate change, inequality, social distrust, all require that we try. But we still have the time to do it. After all, if we look up the next time we are able to be in London, we will see that St. Paul's has not fallen down and the sea has not slid over the Strand. For all of the injustices that beset them, everyday people still live in a country that they know truly belongs to them.

Notes
Acknowledgements
Index

Notes

A *note on sources:* Many of the articles, essays, poems, and broadcasts discussed in this book are now available in various collections as well as in their place of original publication. I have endeavoured where possible to refer to easily accessible, collected versions so as to enable readers to follow up references as straightforwardly as possible.

Introduction

1. George Orwell, *The Lion and the Unicorn: Socialism and the English Genius* (1941), reprinted in *The Collected Essays, Journalism and Letters of George Orwell* (London: Secker and Warburg, 1968), 2:61.

2. J. B. Priestley, *English Journey: Being a Rambling but Truthful Account of What One Man Saw and Heard and Felt and Thought during a Journey through England during the Autumn of the Year 1933* (1934; London: Penguin, 1984), 40.

3. Dylan Thomas, "Swansea and the Arts" (1949), in *On the Air with Dylan Thomas: The Broadcasts*, ed. Ralph Maud (London: New Directions, 1991), 219.

4. Tom Hopkinson, "Bill Brandt, Photographer," *Lilliput* 11, no. 2 (1942): 141.

5. Dylan Thomas to Bert Trick, 29 September 1939, in *Dylan Thomas: The Collected Letters*, ed. Paul Ferris (London: Paladin, 1987), 417.

6. Editors, "Joyful for a Season," *Time*, 14 May 1951, 32; Basil Taylor, *The Official Book of the Festival of Britain, 1951* (London: HMSO, 1951).

7. See Ruth Kenny, Jeff McMillan, and Martin Myrone, *British Folk Art* (London: Tate, 2014).

8. T. S. Eliot, preface to *The Need for Roots: Prelude to a Declaration of Duties towards Mankind*, by Simone Weil (1949; London: Routledge, 1995), xi.

9. None of these accusations are entirely new, of course. For an earlier version of the same account, see Raphael Samuel, *Theatres of Memory*, vol. 2, *Island Stories, Unravelling Britain* (London: Verso, 1998). In the title essay, Samuel declares that "Britain is a term which has a very uncertain future" (41).

10. Richard Rorty, *Achieving Our Country: Leftist Thought in Twentieth-Century America* (Cambridge, MA: Harvard University Press, 1998).

11. Dylan Thomas, "The Festival Exhibition" (1951), in Maud, *On the Air*, 251.

1. Getting Out of the Whale

1. Academic historians, of course, have been largely resistant to this mythmaking. See Angus Calder, *The Myth of the Blitz* (London: Jonathan Cape, 1991); Mark Connelly, *We Can Take It! Britain and the Memory of the Second World War* (Harlow: Longman, 2004); Lucy Noakes and Juliette Pattinson, *British Cultural Memory and the Second World War* (London: Bloomsbury, 2014); and Malcolm Smith, *Britain and 1940: History, Myth and Popular Memory* (London: Routledge, 2000).

2. Dylan Thomas to Bert Trick, 29 September 1939, in *Dylan Thomas: The Collected Letters*, ed. Paul Ferris (London: Paladin, 1987), 416–417.

3. George Orwell, *Inside the Whale* (1939), reprinted in *The Collected Essays, Journalism and Letters of George Orwell* (London: Secker and Warburg, 1968), 1:525.

4. Recent scholars have emphasized that this disillusionment was faster for some intellectuals than for others. See George Robb, *British Culture and the First World War* (London: Palgrave, 2015).

5. Dylan Thomas to Pamela Hansford Johnson, 11 November 1933, in *Collected Letters*, 54.

6. D. H. Lawrence, *Lady Chatterley's Lover* (1933; Cambridge: Cambridge University Press, 2002), 143. See too the discussion in Mark Spilka's excellent collection of early commentaries, Mark Spilka, ed., *D. H. Lawrence: A Collection of Critical Essays* (Englewood Cliffs, NJ: Prentice Hall, 1963).

7. Lawrence, *Lady Chatterley's Lover*, 1.

8. D. H. Lawrence, "England, My England" (1915), reprinted in *D. H. Lawrence: Selected Stories*, ed. Sue Wilson (London: Penguin, 2007), 78–79.

9. D. H. Lawrence, "Democracy" (date unknown), reprinted in *Selected Essays* (London: Penguin, 1950), 80.

10. Lawrence, 94.

11. D. H. Lawrence, "The State of Funk" (1930), reprinted in *Selected Essays*, 99.

12. Lawrence, 96.

13. Orwell, *Inside the Whale*, 507, 509.

14. T. S. Eliot, "The Waste Land" (1922), in *The Waste Land and Other Poems* (London: Penguin, 2003), 82.

15. Raymond Williams, *Culture and Society: Coleridge to Orwell* (London: Hogarth, 1987), 172–173.

16. Lawrence, "State of Funk," 97.

17. D. H. Lawrence, "Nottingham and the Mining Country" (1929,) in *Selected Essays*, 121–122.

18. T. S. Eliot, *After Strange Gods* (London: Harcourt Brace, 1934), 43.

19. H. R. Read, "Democracy and Leadership," *Criterion* 3, no. 9 (1924): 132. See too T. S. Eliot, "*Ulysses*, Order and Myth" (1923), reprinted in *Selected Prose of T. S. Eliot*, ed. Frank Kermode (London: Faber and Faber, 1975), 175–178; and T. S. Eliot, *The Sacred Wood: Essays on Poetry and Criticism* (1920; London: Methuen, 1932).

20. For inspired discussion, see Christopher Hilliard, *English as a Vocation: The Scrutiny Movement* (Oxford: Oxford University Press, 2012). See too F. R. Leavis and Denys Thompson, *Culture and Environment: The Training of Critical Awareness* (London: Chatto and Windus, 1933).

21. Raymond Williams, *Resources of Hope: Culture, Democracy, Socialism* (London: Verso, 1989), 113–114.

22. L. C. Knights, "Will Training Colleges Bear Scrutiny?," *Scrutiny* 1, no. 3 (1932): 259.

23. See Stuart Chase, *A New Deal* (New York: Macmillan, 1932); and Irving Babbitt, *Democracy and Leadership* (New York: Macmillan, 1924).

24. For provocative discussion, see John Carey, *The Intellectuals and the Masses: Pride and Prejudice among the Literary Intelligentsia, 1880–1939* (London: Faber and Faber, 1992).

25. F. R. Leavis, "What's Wrong with Criticism?," *Scrutiny* 1, no. 2 (1932): 145.

26. F. R. Leavis, "Restatements for Critics," *Scrutiny* 1, no. 4 (1933): 322.

27. F. R. Leavis, "The Literary Mind," *Scrutiny* 1, no. 1 (1932): 31.

28. George Sturt, *The Wheelwright's Shop* (Cambridge: Cambridge University Press, 1923).

29. Alexandra Harris, *Romantic Moderns: English Writers, Artists and the Imagination from Virginia Woolf to John Piper* (London: Thames and Hudson, 2010), 142. See too David Matless, *Landscape and Englishness* (London: Reaktion Books, 1998).

30. For a more sceptical take, see Peter Mandler, "'Against Englishness': English Culture and the Limits of Rural Nostalgia, 1850–1940," *Transactions of the Royal Historical Society* 7 (1997): 155–175.

31. *Guide to the Pavilion of the United Kingdom, Australia, New Zealand and the British Colonial Empire* (London: HMSO, 1939), 28.

32. Jed Esty, *A Shrinking Island: Modernism and National Culture in England* (Princeton, NJ: Princeton University Press, 2004), 39.

33. See Martin Hammer, *Graham Sutherland: Landscapes, War Scenes, Portraits, 1924–1950* (London: Scala, 2005); and David Fraser Jenkins, *John Piper* (London: Tate, 1983).

34. See Marion Milner, *A Life of Own's Own* (1934; London: Routledge, 2011). For the influence of this approach on business, literature, and poli-

tics, see Kit Kowol, "An Experiment in Conservative Modernity: Interwar Conservatism and Henry Ford's English Farms," *Journal of British Studies* 55, no. 4 (2016): 781–805; Alison Light, *Forever England: Femininity, Literature and Conservatism between the Wars* (London: Routledge, 1991); and Philip Williamson, *Stanley Baldwin: Conservative Leadership and National Values* (Cambridge: Cambridge University Press, 1999).

35. J. B. Priestley, *English Journey: Being a Rambling but Truthful Account of What One Man Saw and Heard and Felt and Thought during a Journey Through England during the Autumn of the Year 1933* (1934; London: Penguin, 1984), 66.

36. For discussion, see Harris, *Romantic Moderns*, 184; and Dan Stone, "The Far Right and the Back-to-the-Land Movement," in *The Culture of Fascism: Visions of the Far Right in Britain*, ed. Julie Gottlieb and Thomas Linehan (London: I. B. Tauris, 2004).

37. Knights, "Will Training Colleges Bear Scrutiny?," 262.

38. *Guide to the Pavilion*, 24.

39. Orwell, *Inside the Whale*, 509.

40. For excellent discussion, see Ben Jackson, *Equality and the British Left: A Study in Progressive Thought, 1900–1964* (Manchester: Manchester University Press, 2011), esp. 93–150; and Richard Overy, *The Morbid Age: Britain and the Crisis of Civilization, 1919–1939* (London: Penguin, 2009), esp. 50–92. For the roots of these developments, see Mark Bevir, *The Making of British Socialism* (Princeton, NJ: Princeton University Press, 2011).

41. See W. H. Auden, *The English Auden: Poems, Essays and Dramatic Writings, 1927–1939* (London: Faber, 1977); and for good introductory discussions, David Bradshaw, *A Concise Companion to Modernism* (Oxford: Blackwell, 2003), and Valentine Cunningham, *British Writers of the Thirties* (Oxford: Oxford University Press, 1988).

42. Orwell, *Inside the Whale*, 510.

43. F. R. Leavis, "Literature and Society", *Scrutiny* 12, no. 1 (1943): 2.

44. Stephen Spender, *The '30s and After: Poetry, Politics, People, 1930s–1970s* (New York: Random House, 1978), 12–13. See too Stephen Spender, *The Destructive Element: A Study of Modern Writers and Their Beliefs* (London: Cape, 1935).

45. Spender, *'30s and After*, 7.

46. W. H. Auden quoted in Spender, 16.

47. Spender, 49–50.

48. Spender, 17.

49. W. H. Auden, "Spain 1937" (1937), reprinted in *Selected Poems* (London: Faber, 2010), 288.

50. See Spender, *'30s and After*, 19.

51. Orwell, *Inside the Whale*, 510.

52. In a voluminous literature on Orwell, the best discussion on this theme remains Alex Zwerdling, *Orwell and the Left* (New Haven, CT: Yale University Press, 1974), esp. 38–61.

53. Dylan Thomas to Bert Trick, December 1934, in *Collected Letters*, 177.

54. Dylan Thomas to Glyn Jones, 14 March 1934, in *Collected Letters*, 98.

55. Dylan Thomas to Henry Teece, 31 December 1938, in *Collected Letters*, 48.

56. Spender, *'30s and After*, 14.

57. George Orwell, *The Lion and the Unicorn: Socialism and the English Genius* (1941), reprinted in *Collected Essays*, 2:40.

58. D. H. Lawrence, "Insouciance" (1928), in *Selected Essays*, 105.

59. George Orwell, *The Road to Wigan Pier* (1936), reprinted in *The Complete Longer Non-fiction of George Orwell* (London: Penguin, 1983), 264.

60. Orwell, 266.

61. Orwell, *Inside the Whale*, 162.

62. Spender, *'30s and After*, 12.

63. Spender, 34.

64. Spender, 12.

65. Orwell, *Inside the Whale*, 526.

66. Orwell, *Inside the Whale*, 528.

67. Orwell, *Lion and the Unicorn*, 93.

2. A Little Holding of Ground

1. Harvey Perkins and David Thomas, *Place, Identity and Everyday Life in a Globalizing World* (Basingstoke: Palgrave, 2012), 1. For more accessible recent analyses of the everyday, see Joseph A. Amato, *Everyday Life: How the Ordinary Became Extraordinary* (London: Reaktion, 2016); and Ben

Highmore, *Ordinary Lives: Studies in the Everyday* (London: Routledge, 2011).

2. Henri Lefebvre, *The Critique of Everyday Life* (1947; London: Verso, 2014), 21.

3. George Orwell, *Coming Up for Air* (1939; London: Penguin, 2000), 166.

4. George Orwell, *Inside the Whale* (1939), reprinted in *The Collected Essays, Journalism and Letters of George Orwell* (London: Secker and Warburg, 1968), 1:497.

5. Orwell, 499.

6. John Carey, *The Intellectuals and the Masses: Pride and Prejudice among the Literary Intelligentsia, 1880–1939* (London: Faber and Faber, 1992), 8.

7. D. H. Lawrence, *Apocalypse* (1930; New York: Viking, 1960), 32.

8. D. H. Lawrence, "Insouciance" (1928), in *Selected Essays* (London: Penguin, 1950), 104–105.

9. Lawrence, 106.

10. D. H. Lawrence, "Dull London" (1928), in *Selected Essays*, 124–125.

11. Orwell, *Coming Up for Air*, 1.

12. Orwell, 173.

13. Orwell, 172.

14. E. M. Forster, "George Orwell" (1950), reprinted in *Two Cheers for Democracy* (London: Penguin, 1978), 70.

15. Orwell, *Coming Up for Air*, 173.

16. George Orwell, *The Road to Wigan Pier* (1936), reprinted in *The Complete Longer Non-fiction of George Orwell* (London: Penguin, 1983), 282.

17. Priestley's childhood and early adulthood are beautifully evoked in Diana Collins, *Time and the Priestleys: The Story of a Friendship* (Stroud: Allan Sutton, 1994), 37–48.

18. J. B. Priestley, *Delight* (1949; Ilkley: Great Northern Books, 2009), 64.

19. J. B. Priestley, *English Journey: Being a Rambling but Truthful Account of What One Man Saw and Heard and Felt and Thought during a Journey through England during the Autumn of the Year 1933* (1934; London: Penguin, 1984), 63. It is striking to compare the generosity of Priestley's message here with the tone of the best-selling H. V. Morton, *In Search of England* (London: Methuen, 1927).

20. Priestley, *English Journey*, 184.

21. Priestley, 388.

22. Priestley, 376.

23. Priestley, 41.

24. Priestley, 379.

25. Priestley, 376.

26. Priestley, 252–253.

27. Priestley, 86.

28. Priestley, 86.

29. Priestley, 377.

30. See James Hinton, *Nine Wartime Lives: Mass Observation and the Making of the Modern Self* (Oxford: Oxford University Press, 2010).

31. Priestley, *English Journey*, 374.

32. Priestley, 390.

33. For a superb account, see Andrew Lycett, *Dylan Thomas: A New Life* (London: Phoenix, 2003).

34. William Empson quoted in John Goodby, *The Poetry of Dylan Thomas: Under the Spelling Wall* (Liverpool: Liverpool University Press, 2013), 50.

35. Dylan Thomas to Glyn Jones, 14 March 1934, in *Dylan Thomas: The Collected Letters*, ed. Paul Ferris (London: Paladin, 1987), 97.

36. Dylan Thomas to Pamela Hansford Johnson, 15 October 1933, in *Collected Letters*, 27.

37. Dylan Thomas to Richard Church, 1 May 1936, in *Collected Letters*, 227.

38. Dylan Thomas to David Higham, 9 February 1937, in *Collected Letters*, 245.

39. Dylan Thomas to Pamela Hansford Johnson, 15 April 1934, in *Collected Letters*, 111.

40. Dylan Thomas to Pamela Hansford Johnson, November 1933, in *Collected Letters*, 41.

41. Dylan Thomas to Pamela Hansford Johnson, 25 December 1933, in *Collected Letters*, 74–75.

42. Dylan Thomas to Pamela Hansford Johnson, 21 May 1934, in *Collected Letters*, 139.

43. Dylan Thomas, "Holiday Memory" (1946), in *On the Air with Dylan Thomas: The Broadcasts*, ed. Ralph Maud (London: New Directions, 1991), 141.

44. Dylan Thomas to Bert Trick, 29 September 1939, in *Dylan Thomas: The Collected Letters*, ed. Paul Ferris (London: Paladin, 1987), 417.

45. Dylan Thomas, "Extraordinary Little Cough" (1940), reprinted in *Collected Stories* (London: Weidenfeld and Nicolson, 2014), 177.

46. W. H. Mellers, "The Bard and the Prep-School," *Scrutiny* 9, no. 1 (1940): 77.

3. The Properties of My Memory Remain

1. See discussion in Malcolm Smith, *Britain and 1940: History, Myth and Popular Memory* (London: Routledge, 2000); and Daniel Todman, *Britain's War: Into Battle, 1937–1941* (New York: Oxford University Press, 2016).

2. As mentioned earlier, professional historians are largely immune to the charms of these myths. In addition to those already cited, see Nicholas Harman, *Dunkirk and the Patriotic Myth* (New York: Simon and Schuster, 1980); and Clive Ponting, *1940: Myth and Reality* (London: Hamish Hamilton, 1940).

3. George Orwell, *Coming Up for Air* (1939; London: Penguin, 2000), 166.

4. Dylan Thomas to Vernon Watkins, summer 1940, in *Dylan Thomas: The Collected Letters*, ed. Paul Ferris (London: Paladin, 1987), 463.

5. George Orwell, *The Road to Wigan Pier* (1936), reprinted in *The Complete Longer Non-Fiction of George Orwell* (London: Penguin, 1983), 279.

6. See David Fraser Jenkins, *John Piper: The Forties* (London: Imperial War Museum, 2000); and Martin Hammer, *Graham Sutherland: Landscapes, War Scenes, Portraits 1927–1950* (London: Scalia, 2006).

7. Cyril Connolly, editorial, *Horizon* 1, no. 1 (1939): 3.

8. George Orwell [John Freeman, pseud.], "Can Socialists Be Happy?" (1943), Orwell Foundation, https://www.orwellfoundation.com/the-orwell -foundation/orwell/essays-and-other-works/can-socialists-be-happy/. For a powerful in-depth analysis of this essay, see Alex Woloch, *Or Orwell: Writing*

and Democratic Socialism (Cambridge, MA: Harvard University Press, 2016), 304–315.

9. Dylan Thomas to Henry Teece, 6 July 1938, in *Collected Letters*, 310.

10. J. B. Priestley, *Postscripts* (London: William Heinemann, 1940), vii.

11. George Orwell, *The Lion and the Unicorn: Socialism and the English Genius* (1941), reprinted in *The Collected Essays, Journalism and Letters of George Orwell* (London: Secker and Warburg, 1968), 2:61.

12. D. H. Lawrence, "Democracy" (date unknown), reprinted in *Selected Essays* (London: Penguin, 1950), 88–89.

13. Bonnie Honig, *Public Things: Democracy in Disrepair* (New York: Fordham University Press, 2017), 56.

14. George Orwell, "Frontiers in Art and Propaganda" (1941), reprinted in *Seeing Things as They Are: Selected Journalism and Other Writings* (London: Hervill Secker, 2014), 145. This was a characteristic Orwellian response to a literary giant, as explored in Stefan Collini, *Absent Minds: Intellectuals in Britain* (Oxford: Oxford University Press, 2006), 350–372.

15. Virginia Woolf, "Modern Fiction" (1925), in *The Essays of Virginia Woolf*, ed. Andrew McNellie (London: Hogarth, 1994), 4:160. See the excellent discussion in Rachel Bowlby, *Everyday Stories* (Oxford: Oxford University Press, 2016), esp. 134–135.

16. For thoroughgoing communitarian readings of *Between the Acts*, see Jed Esty, *A Shrinking Island: Modernism and National Culture in England* (Princeton, NJ: Princeton University Press, 2004), esp. 39–45; and Alexandra Harris, *Romantic Moderns: English Writers, Artists and the Imagination from Virginia Woolf to John Piper* (London: Thames and Hudson, 2010), esp. 109–114.

17. Virginia Woolf, *Between the Acts* (1941; London: Penguin, 1992), 64.

18. Woolf, 68.

19. Woolf, 105.

20. Woolf, 109.

21. Woolf, 104.

22. Woolf, 116–117.

23. Priestley, *Postscripts*, 61.

24. Dylan Thomas to Vernon Watkins, 13 December 1939, in *Collected Letters*, 434.

25. Laurie Lee, "Invasion Summer" (1940), reprinted in *Selected Poems* (Chicago: University of Chicago Press, 2014), 2.

26. Orwell, *Lion and the Unicorn*, 57.

27. George Orwell, "War Begins at Home" (1940), reprinted in *Seeing Things as They Are*, 82.

28. George Orwell, "On Preparation for Imminent Invasion" (1940), reprinted in *Seeing Things as They Are*, 104.

29. Orwell, of course, was not alone in this view, which owed much to the advocacy of Tom Witringham. See especially Tom Witringham, *New Ways of War* (London: Penguin, 1940).

30. Priestley, *Postscripts*, 11.

31. Priestley, 25.

32. Priestley, 12.

33. Priestley, 68.

34. Priestley, 74.

35. Priestley, 20.

36. Priestley, 80.

37. Priestley, 33.

38. Priestley, 2.

39. Priestley, 2.

40. Priestley, 2–3.

41. Dylan Thomas to Clement Davenport, 23 April 1941, in *Collected Letters*, 481.

42. Dylan Thomas, "Among Those Killed in the Dawn Raid Was a Man Aged a Hundred" (1941), reprinted in *Collected Poems, 1934–1953* (London: Weidenfeld and Nicolson, 2000), 112.

43. Honig, *Public Things*, 65.

44. Dylan Thomas, "Reminiscences of Childhood" (1943), reprinted in *On the Air with Dylan Thomas: The Broadcasts*, ed. Ralph Maud (London: New Directions, 1991), 6.

45. Thomas, 6.

46. Thomas, 7.

47. Thomas, 3, 8.

48. Thomas, "Living in Wales" (1949), reprinted in Maud, *On the Air,* 205.

49. Marilynne Robinson, *When I Was a Child I Read Books* (London: Virago, 2012), 20–21.

50. See Andrew Lycett, *Dylan Thomas: A New Life* (London: Phoenix, 2003), 261.

51. Dylan Thomas, "Fern Hill" (1945), reprinted in *Collected Poems,* 134.

52. Orwell, *Coming Up for Air,* 27.

53. Thomas, "Reminiscences of Childhood," 3.

4. All Nations Are Odious, but Some Are Less Odious Than Others

1. Bill Brandt, *The English at Home* (London: Batsford, 1936); Bill Brandt, *A Night in London* (London: Country Life, 1938).

2. Stephen Brooke, "War and the Nude: The Photography of Bill Brandt in the 1940s," *Journal of British Studies* 45, no. 1 (2006): 118–138.

3. This mixed sentiment was also a commonplace in wartime literature. See, for a classic example, Elizabeth Bowen, *The Heat of the Day* (1948; London: Vintage, 1998); and for discussion, Peter Stansky and William Abrahams, *London's Burning: Life, Death and Art in the Second World War* (London: Constable, 1994).

4. Tom Hopkinson, "Bill Brandt," *Lilliput* 11, no. 2 (1942): 130.

5. Brandt quoted in John Szarkowski, "Bill Brandt," *Members Newsletter, Museum of Modern Art* 6, no. 3 (1969): 11–12.

6. George Orwell, *The Lion and the Unicorn: Socialism and the English Genius* (1941), reprinted in *The Collected Essays, Journalism and Letters of George Orwell* (London: Secker and Warburg, 1968), 2:61.

7. Dylan Thomas to Trevor Hughes, February 1933, reprinted in *Dylan Thomas: The Collected Letters,* ed. Paul Ferris (London: Paladin, 1987), 12.

8. Dylan Thomas to Pamela Hansford Johnson, November 1933, in *Collected Letters,* 43.

9. Orwell, *Lion and the Unicorn,* 61.

10. J. B. Priestley, *English Journey: Being a Rambling but Truthful Account of What One Man Saw and Heard and Felt and Thought during a Journey through*

England during the Autumn of the Year 1933 (1934; London: Penguin, 1984), 389.

11. Orwell, *Lion and the Unicorn*, 57.

12. Thomas, "Reminiscences of Childhood," reprinted in *On the Air with Dylan Thomas: The Broadcasts*, ed. Ralph Maud (London: New Directions, 1991), 3.

13. Priestley, *English Journey*, 260.

14. Orwell, *Lion and the Unicorn*, 65.

15. Orwell, 56.

16. Brooke, "War and the Nude," 119.

17. Dylan Thomas, *Conquest of a Germ* (1943), reprinted in *The Filmscripts* (London: J. M. Dent, 1995), 101.

18. Dylan Thomas, *Our Country* (1944), reprinted in *Filmscripts*, 72.

19. Thomas, 68.

20. Angus Calder, *The People's War: Britain, 1939–1945* (London: Pimlico, 1992).

21. Sonya Rose, *Which People's War? National Identity and Citizenship in Britain, 1939–1945* (Oxford: Oxford University Press, 2003), 286, 2.

22. There would have been plenty of opportunities for such discussion too. See Wendy Webster, *Mixing It: Diversity in World War Two Britain* (Oxford: Oxford University Press, 2018).

23. Priestley, *English Journey*, 389.

24. Orwell, *Lion and the Unicorn*, 61.

25. Orwell, 59.

26. Thomas, *Our Country*, 67.

27. Orwell, *Lion and the Unicorn*, 59.

28. J. B. Priestley, *Out of the People* (London: Collins, 1941), 99.

29. Orwell, *Lion and the Unicorn*, 16.

30. J. B. Priestley, *Postscripts* (London: William Heinemann, 1940), 7.

31. Priestley, 20–21.

32. Simone Weil, *The Need for Roots: Prelude to a Declaration of Duties towards Mankind* (1949; London: Routledge, 1995), 41.

33. Dylan Thomas, "What Has Happened to English Poetry?" (1946), reprinted in Maud, *On the Air*, 134.

34. Orwell, *Lion and the Unicorn*, 56.

35. Paul Delany, *Bill Brandt: A Life* (London: Jonathan Cape, 2003), 124.

36. Thomas, *Our Country*, 67.

37. Dylan Thomas, *Under Milk Wood* (1954), reprinted in *The Dylan Thomas Omnibus: Under Milk Wood, Poems, Stories and Broadcasts* (London: Phoenix, 2004), 327.

38. Orwell, *Lion and the Unicorn*, 86.

39. Orwell, 56, 93.

40. Dylan Thomas, *These Are the Men* (1944), reprinted in *Filmscripts*, 40.

41. Dylan Thomas, *Unconquerable People* (1944), reprinted in *Filmscripts*, 61.

42. Priestley, *Postscripts*, 73.

43. E. M. Forster, "George Orwell" (1950), reprinted in *Two Cheers for Democracy* (London: Penguin, 1978), 71.

44. Dylan Thomas, *Battle for Freedom* (1943), reprinted in *Filmscripts*, 37, 34.

45. George Orwell, "Shooting an Elephant" (1936), reprinted in *The Collected Essays, Journalism and Letters of George Orwell* (London: Secker and Warburg, 1968), 2:235–242.

46. George Orwell, "As I Please" (28 July 1944), reprinted in *The Collected Essays, Journalism and Letters of George Orwell* (London, Secker and Warburg, 1968), 2:199.

47. Orwell, *Lion and the Unicorn*, 62.

48. Priestley, *English Journey*, 389.

49. Dylan Thomas, "Holiday Memory" (1946), reprinted in Maud, *On the Air*, 141.

50. Orwell, *Lion and the Unicorn*, 65.

51. Priestley, *English Journey*, 228.

52. Priestley, 235–236.

53. Fiona Stafford, *Local Attachments: The Province of Poetry* (Oxford: Oxford University Press, 2010), 276–277.

5. The Socialists in Power

1. Clement R. Attlee, *As It Happened* (London: W. Heinemann, 1954).

2. For a paradigmatic case among the many contemporary examples, see G. D. H. Cole, *The Intelligent Man's Guide to the Post-war World* (London:

Victor Gollancz, 1947). For a good overview, see Jim Fyrth, ed., *Labour's Promise Land? Culture and Society in Labour Britain, 1945–51* (London: Lawrence and Wishart, 1995).

3. See Ian Jeffry, *Bill Brandt: Photographs, 1928–1983* (London: Thames and Hudson, 1993), 11, 55; and Stephen Brooke, "War and the Nude: The Photography of Bill Brandt in the 1940s," *Journal of British Studies* 45, no. 1 (2006).

4. Laurie Lee, *Cider with Rosie* (1959), reprinted in *Red Sky at Sunrise* (London: Penguin, 1993); Valerie Grove, *Laurie Lee: The Well-Loved Stranger* (London: Penguin, 2000), esp. 219.

5. J. B. Priestley, editorial, *Sunday Pictorial*, 23 January 1949, 4.

6. Dylan Thomas to Oscar Williams, 30 July 1945, in *Dylan Thomas: The Collected Letters*, ed. Paul Ferris (London: Paladin, 1987), 557.

7. J. B. Priestley, *Out of the People* (London: Collins, 1941), 102, 101.

8. Dylan Thomas to Pamela Hansford Johnson, 25 December 1933, in *Collected Letters*, 76.

9. See Clarisse Bethezene, *Training Minds for the War of Ideas: Ashridge College, the Conservative Party and the Cultural Politics of Britain, 1929–54* (Manchester: Manchester University Press, 2015); Reba Soffer, *History, Historians, and Conservatism in Britain and America: From the Great War to Thatcher and Reagan* (Oxford: Oxford University Press, 2009); and Julia Stapleton, *Sir Arthur Bryant and National History in Twentieth-Century Britain* (Lanham, MD: Lexington Books, 2005).

10. D. H. Lawrence, *Kangaroo* (1922; London: Penguin, 1988), 113.

11. D. H. Lawrence, "Democracy" (date unknown), reprinted in *Selected Essays* (London: Penguin, 1950), 78.

12. George Orwell, "Preface to Animal Farm" (1945), reprinted in *The Collected Essays, Journalism and Letters of George Orwell* (London: Secker and Warburg, 1968), 3:404.

13. George Orwell, "Politics and the English Language" (1946), reprinted in *Why I Write* (London: Penguin, 2004), 111.

14. Orwell, 120.

15. Orwell, 118.

16. George Orwell, *The Road to Wigan Pier* (1936), reprinted in *The Complete Longer Non- Fiction of George Orwell* (London: Penguin, 1983), 291.

17. George Orwell, *The Lion and the Unicorn: Socialism and the English Genius* (1941), reprinted in *The Collected Essays, Journalism and Letters of George Orwell* (London: Secker and Warburg, 1968), 2:79.

18. George Orwell, *"The Road to Serfdom and Mirror of the Past"* (1944), reprinted in *Collected Essays*, 3:119.

19. George Orwell [John Freeman, pseud.], "Can Socialists Be Happy?" (1943), Orwell Foundation, https://www.orwellfoundation.com/the-orwell-foundation/orwell/essays-and-other-works/can-socialists-be-happy/.

20. Orwell.

21. Orwell quoted in David Kynaston, *Austerity Britain, 1945–51* (London: Bloomsbury, 2007), 174.

22. George Orwell, *Nineteen Eighty-Four* (1949; London: Penguin, 2017).

23. Raymond Williams, *Orwell* (London: Fontana, 1991), 79.

24. Bernard Crick, *"Nineteen Eighty-Four:* Context and Controversy," in *The Cambridge Companion to George Orwell*, ed. John Rodden (Cambridge: Cambridge University Press, 2007), 152. This interpretation is pushed to its furthest extreme in John Newsinger, *Hope Lies in the Proles: George Orwell and the Left* (London: Pluto, 2018).

25. Dylan Thomas, "Memories of Christmas" (1945), reprinted in *On the Air with Dylan Thomas: The Broadcasts*, ed. Ralph Maud (London: New Directions, 1991), 22.

26. Dylan Thomas to Pamela Hansford Johnson, 11 November 1933, in *Collected Letters*, 55–57.

27. Dylan Thomas to Henry Teece, 31 December 1938, in *Collected Letters*, 348–349.

28. Dylan Thomas to Harry Klopper, 30 May 1946, in *Collected Letters*, 591.

29. Dylan Thomas to Oscar Williams, 30 July 1945, in *Collected Letters*, 557.

30. Dylan Thomas, *The Londoner* (1946), reprinted in Maud, *On the Air*, 76–77. The broadcast was, of course, a satire of publications like Patrick Abercrombie, *Greater London Plan* (London: HMSO, 1945), and Flora Stephenson and Phoebe Pool, *A Plan for Town and Country* (London: Pilot, 1945), and the documentary films made to publicize them, as captured on BFI, *Land of Promise: The Documentary Film Movement, 1930–1950* (London: BFI, 2009).

31. Dylan Thomas to Princess Caetani, 28 May 1951, in *Collected Letters*, 800.

32. Dylan Thomas to Princess Caetani, October 1951, in *Collected Letters*, 813–814.

33. Thomas to Caetani, 814.

34. Dylan Thomas, *Under Milk Wood* (1954), reprinted in *The Dylan Thomas Omnibus: Under Milk Wood, Poems, Stories and Broadcasts* (London: Phoenix Press, 2004), 343.

35. Thomas, 344.

36. Thomas, 342.

37. Thomas, 328.

38. Thomas, 343.

39. Thomas to Caetani, October 1951, 814.

40. Dylan Thomas, "Laugharne" (1951), reprinted in Maud, *On the Air*, 364.

6. Brief City

1. Peter Mair, *Ruling the Void: The Hollowing of Western Democracy* (London: Verso, 2013).

2. Personal notes.

3. Basil Taylor, *The Official Book of the Festival of Britain, 1951* (London: HMSO, 1951), 3.

4. Gerald Barry quoted in Harriet Atkinson, *The Festival of Britain: A Land and Its People* (London: I. B. Tauris, 2012), 8.

5. For excellent overviews, see Mary Banham and Bevis Hillier, eds., *A Tonic to the Nation: The Festival of Britain 1951* (London: Thames and Hudson, 1976); Becky E. Conekin, *"The Autobiography of a Nation": The 1951 Festival of Britain* (Manchester: Manchester University Press, 2003); Elain Harwood and Alan Powers, eds., *Festival of Britain* (London: Twentieth Century Society, 2001); Charlotte Mullins, *A Festival on the River: The Story of the Southbank Centre* (London: Penguin, 2007); and Paul Rennie, *Festival of Britain Design, 1951* (London: Antique Collectors' Club, 2007).

6. See *Daily Mail: A Festival Supplement*, May 1951.

7. See Jim English, "Empire Day in Britain, 1904–1958," *Historical Journal* 49, no. 1 (2006): 247–276; and Peter Hoffenberg, *An Empire on Display:*

English, Indian, and Australian Exhibitions from the Crystal Palace to the Great War (Berkeley: University of California Press, 2001).

8. Roy Strong, "Utopia Limited," in Banham and Hillier, *Tonic to the Nation*, 7.

9. Hugh Casson in Jacques B. Brunius and Maurice Harvey, dirs., *Brief City*, written by Patrick O'Donovan (1951), https://media.nationalarchives .gov.uk/index.php/brief-city/.

10. See Mary Shoeser, "The Application of Science," in Harwood and Powers, *Festival of Britain*, 117–126.

11. Hugh Casson, "South Bank Sculpture," *Image* 7 (1952): 57.

12. Raphael Samuel, *Theatres of Memory*, vol. 1, *Past and Present in Contemporary Culture* (London: Verso, 1994), 56, 58.

13. See Valerie Grove, *Laurie Lee: The Well-Loved Stranger* (London: Penguin, 2000), 252–260; and Barbara Jones, "Popular Art," in Banham and Hillier, *Tonic to the Nation*, 129–132.

14. Taylor, *Official Book*, 3.

15. Gerald Barry, "Tonic to the Nation," in *Daily Mail: Festival Supplement*, 5.

16. Casson in Brunius and Harvey, *Brief City*.

17. See Editors, "Festival Diary," *New Statesman and Nation*, 5 May 1951, 497.

18. Casson in Brunius and Harvey, *Brief City*.

19. Casson. See too Hugh Casson, "Adventure on the South Bank," in *Festival of Britain Preview and Guide* (London: HMSO, 1951).

20. See H. T. Cadbury-Brown, "A Good Time-and-a-Half Was Had by All," in Harwood and Powers, *Festival of Britain*, 59–64.

21. Dylan Thomas, "The Festival Exhibition" (1951), reprinted in *On the Air with Dylan Thomas: The Broadcasts*, ed. Ralph Maud (London: New Directions, 1991), 248, 249.

22. Thomas, 247.

23. Hugh Casson, "Adventure on the South Bank," in *Festival of Britain Preview and Guide* (London: HMSO, 1951), 3.

24. James Tully, *Public Philosophy in a New Key*, vol. 1, *Democracy and Civic Freedom* (Cambridge: Cambridge University Press, 2008), 137.

25. See Mullins, *Festival on the River*, 54; and Rennie, *Festival of Britain*, 32.

26. Alan Powers, "The Expression of Levity," in Harwood and Powers, *Festival of Britain*, 55.

27. G. S. Whittet, "Encouragement for Artists," in Banham and Hillier, *Tonic to the Nation*, 182.

28. See South Bank Centre, "Festival Memories," accessed August 2009, http://www.southbankcentre.co.uk/festival-memories/, contributions by French, Ahmed, Reid, and Sunderland. At the time of writing, the page is no longer available, as the archive is being recatalogued. For updates, see https://www.southbankcentre.co.uk/venues/archive-studio.

29. James Gardner, "Battersea Pleasures," in Banham and Hillier, *Tonic to the Nation*, 122.

30. South Bank Centre, "Festival Memories."

31. Barry, "Tonic to the Nation," 5.

32. George Murray, "Lion and the Unicorn," in *Daily Mail: Festival Supplement*, 16.

33. J. B. Priestley, "The Renewed Dream of Merrie England," *New York Times*, 15 July 1951.

34. Tully, *Public Philosophy*, 137. Also see Johan Huizinga, *Homo Ludens: A Study of the Play Element in Culture* (1944; London: Routledge and Kegan Paul, 1950).

35. Margaret Lambert and Enid Marx, *English Popular Art* (London: R. T. Batsford, 1951), vii.

36. Barbara Jones, *The Unsophisticated Arts* (London: Architectural, 1951), 9.

37. Jones, 9.

38. Jones, 10.

39. Jones, 10.

40. Jones, 11.

41. Taylor, *Official Book*, 70.

42. Cover material, *The About Britain Guides* (London: William Collins, 1951).

43. Taylor, *Official Book*, 65.

44. Taylor, 65.

45. J. B. Priestley, *Festival at Farbridge* (London: Macmillan, 1951).

46. Barry, "Tonic to the Nation," 5.

47. See Rennie, *Festival of Britain*, 24.

48. Antony D. Hippisley Coxe, "I Enjoyed It More Than Anything in My Life," in Banham and Hillier, *Tonic to the Nation*, 89.

49. Kenneth O. Morgan, *Labour in Power, 1945–1951* (Oxford: Oxford University Press, 1985), 503.

50. Ian Cox, *The South Bank Exhibition: A Guide to the Story It Tells* (London: HMSO, 1951), i.

51. See Cox, ii–xxxvii; and *Daily Mail: Festival Supplement*, 5, 7, 9, 10, 46.

52. See Gardner, "Battersea Pleasures."

53. See Becky Conekin, "Fun and Fantasy, Escape and Edification: The Battersea Pleasure Gardens," in Harwood and Powers, *Festival of Britain*, 132–133.

54. "Pleasure Gardens," in *Daily Mail: Festival Supplement*, 53.

55. South Bank Centre, "Festival Memories."

56. Stephen Spender, *The '30s and After: Poetry, Politics, People, 1930s–1970s* (New York: Random House, 1978), 75.

57. Strong, "Utopia Limited," 8.

58. Strong, 8.

59. Priestley, "Renewed Dream."

60. Jones, *Unsophisticated Arts*, 171.

61. Marghanita Laski quoted in Bevis Hillier, introduction to Banham and Hillier, *Tonic to the Nation*, 11.

7. Acquaintance plus Wonder

1. For an excellent account of what stayed and what was lost in the years after the Clement Attlee government, see John Grindrod, *Concretopia: A Journey around the Rebuilding of Postwar Britain* (London: Old Street, 2013). For a persuasive theoretical account of the recent changes, see Wendy Brown, *Undoing the Demos: Neoliberalism's Stealth Revolution* (New York: Zone Books, 2015).

2. For excellent overviews of the context in the UK, see Ben Jackson, "Hard Labour," *Political Quarterly* 87, no. 21 (2016): 3–5; and Lewis Goodall, *Left for Dead? The Strange Death and Rebirth of the Labour Party* (London: William Collins, 2018).

3. Chantal Mouffe, *For a Left Populism* (London: Verso, 2018), 93.

4. See Adam Phillips, *Unforbidden Pleasures* (New York: Picador, 2015). For a fascinating connection between this idea and the ideas at the heart of events like the Festival of Britain, see Pierre Huyghe, *Celebration Park* (London: Tate, 2006).

5. Phillips, *Unforbidden Pleasures*, 126.

6. Phillips, 162.

7. Phillips, 195.

8. Andrew Abbott, "Aims of Education," University of Chicago, 2002, https://college.uchicago.edu/student-life/aims-education-address-2002 -andrew-abbott.

9. Abbott.

10. Dylan Thomas to Henry Teece, 6 July 1938, in *Dylan Thomas: The Collected Letters*, ed. Paul Ferris (London: Paladin, 1987), 310.

11. For an excellent introduction to community organizing of the Citizens UK form, see Luke Bretherton, *Resurrecting Democracy: Faith, Citizenship and the Politics of a Common Life* (Cambridge: Cambridge University Press, 2015).

12. Raymond Williams, *The Politics of Modernism: Against the New Conformists* (London: Verso, 2006), 116.

13. Anthony Costello, *The Social Edge: The Power of Sympathy Groups for Our Health, Wealth and Sustainable Future* (London: Thornwick, 2018), 450.

14. For a sampling, see Jørn Tomter's homepage, accessed 11 May 2020, https://tomter.net.

15. See the Every One, Every Day homepage, accessed 11 May 2020, https://www.weareeveryone.org.

16. George Monbiot, "Could This Local Experiment Be the Start of a National Transformation?," *Guardian*, 24 January 2019.

17. Dawn Austwick, "Putting People in the Lead," National Lottery Community Fund blog, 24 March 2015, https://bigblog.org.uk/2015/03/24 /people-in-the-lead/; Hilary Cottam, *Radical Help: How We Can Remake the Relationships between Us and Revolutionise the Welfare State* (London: Virago, 2019); and Adam Lent and Jessica Studdert, *The Community Paradigm: Why Public Services Need Radical Change and How It Can Be Achieved* (London: New Local Government Network, 2019), http://www.nlgn.org.uk/public/wp -content/uploads/The-Community-Paradigm_FINAL.pdf.

18. David Brooks, "The Big Story You Don't Read About," *New York Times*, 16 May 2019. For recent theoretical examination of these themes, see Michael Ignatieff, *The Ordinary Virtues: Moral Order in a Divided World* (Cambridge, MA: Harvard University Press, 2017); and Nancy Rosenblum, *Good Neighbours: The Democracy of Everyday Life in America* (Princeton, NJ: Princeton University Press, 2016).

19. For Ed Miliband, see Rob Merrick, "UK Must Fight Climate Change on 'War Footing' like Defeat of Nazis, Theresa May Told," *Independent,* 29 April 2019, https://www.independent.co.uk/news/uk/politics/uk-climate -change-theresa-may-environment-protest-lucas-ed-miliband-second -world-war-nazis-a8891801.html; and Greta Thunberg, "Our House Is on Fire," *Guardian*, 26 January 2019.

Conclusion

1. Kathleen Stewart, *Ordinary Affects* (Durham, NC: Duke University Press, 2007), 18–19.

2. For similar stories, see Tim Dee, ed., *Ground Work: Writings on Places and People* (London: Penguin, 2018).

3. George Orwell, *Coming Up for Air* (1939; London: Penguin, 2000), 173.

4. Dylan Thomas, *Under Milk Wood* (1954), reprinted in *The Dylan Thomas Omnibus: Under Milk Wood, Poems, Stories and Broadcasts* (London: Phoenix Press, 2004), 304.

5. Barbara Jones, *The Unsophisticated Arts* (London: Architectural Press, 1951), 16.

6. Sheldon Wolin, "The Ordinance of Time," in *Fugitive Democracy and Other Essays* (Princeton, NJ: Princeton University Press, 2016), 258.

7. See Jon Lawrence, *Me, Me, Me: The Search for Community in Post-war Britain* (Oxford: Oxford University Press, 2019); and Eric Klinenberg, *Palaces for the People: How to Build a More Equal and United Society* (London: Penguin, 2018).

8. Danielle Allen, "Toward a Connected Society," in *Our Compelling Interests: The Value of Diversity for Democracy and a Prosperous Society*, ed. E. Lewis and N. Cantor (Princeton, NJ: Princeton University Press, 2016). See

too Danielle Allen, *Talking to Strangers: Anxieties of Citizenship since "Brown versus Board of Education"* (Chicago: University of Chicago Press, 2004).

9. Zadie Smith, "Elegy for a Country's Seasons," in *Feel Free* (London: Hamish Hamilton, 2018), 19.

10. Bonnie Honig, *Public Things: Democracy in Disrepair* (New York: Fordham University Press, 2017), 82, 74. See too Astra Taylor, *Democracy May Not Exist, but We'll Miss It When It's Gone* (New York: Metropolitan, 2019), 276–306. A profound statement of the alternative view, which emphasizes the impossibility of "living in the past," is found in Jonathan Lear, *Radical Hope: Ethics in the Face of Cultural Devastation* (Cambridge, MA: Harvard University Press, 2006).

Acknowledgements

This book has been a long time in the writing, having been interrupted by a general election, Brexit, turmoil in the UK Labour Party, a move to Australia, and a global pandemic. My first and most heartfelt thanks are therefore to my patient and phenomenally insightful editor, Ian Malcolm, and my unparalleled agent, Catherine Clarke. They did not deserve to wait so long, but at each step of the way they have improved the text with suggestions big and small. I am very grateful too for the thoughts of three anonymous reviewers for Harvard University Press; their responses were the perfect combination of generous and challenging, and they improved the manuscript significantly. The editorial team have also been wonderful.

In the time I worked on the book, I was lucky to work in some inspiring places and receive some exceptional gifts. The libraries and colleges of Oxford University still give me goose bumps over thirty years after I first walked in them, and it was similarly uplifting to work, even if just for a brief while, in the beautiful library at the Museo Reina Sofía in Madrid. When I was working for the Labour Party, the brilliant staff at the Houses of Parliament put up rows and rows of bookshelves in my office to enable me to at least keep reading a bit, much to the amusement of my more street-fighting political colleagues. The librarians at Macquarie University then paradoxically helped me get my head back into England when I first arrived in Australia. The exceptional team at the Sydney Policy Lab later encouraged and inspired me every day and kept the whole show on the road when I disappeared to finish the text. I also note with gratitude that initial funding for the project came from the UK's Arts and Humanities Research Council and from the Department of Politics and International Relations, University of Oxford and University College, Oxford, without whose support it would never have got off the ground.

I have been just as lucky in the inspiring conversations had over the long period that I have been working on this book. At the risk of leaving some equally crucial ones out, I do wish to remember some explicitly. Danielle Allen pushed me to show that the very best in political philosophy could live side by side with the most effective political organizing; Tom Baldwin asked me to write until he could "smell the woodbines," which I have tried my best to do; Maurice Glasman and Arnie Graf together taught me that relationships precede action; Cori Hayden reassured me that hard thinking and clear argument always take time; Bonnie Honig helped me hold back my suburban sensibilities just enough to keep my radicalism alive; Will Somerville noted how to combine the freedom of cosmopolitanism with the spirit of belonging; Kit Kowol reminded me both just how exciting Britain in the 1940s was and that radical conservatism is not a contradiction in terms; Jon Stokes asked how we could have a more positive politics; and Amanda Tattersall excited me about community organizing all over again when I arrived in Sydney.

Many other scholars, journalists, campaigners, and politicians, of course, have generously commented on the ideas in the book in seminars, conferences, and workshops. I remember with particular fondness talks at Australian National, Cambridge, Harvard, Oxford, Macquarie, Nottingham, and Sydney Universities. I thank all the participants very much and apologize where my responses have been inadequate. I am also delighted to recall intense discussions with Stefan Baskerville, Duncan Bell, Will Brett, Tessy Britton, Maureen Cole-Burns, Graeme Cooke, Jason Cowley, Jon Cruddas, Sarah Cutler, Jo Day, Jonathan Derbyshire, George Eaton, Sarah Fine, Michael Freeden, Kathy Harvey, Mathew Humphrey, Ben Jackson, Paul Jamieson, Richard Jolly, Gavin Kelly, Desmond King, Rachel Laurence, Caroline Mason, John Mulligan, Lisa Nandy, Nick Pearce, Andrew Pendleton, Steve Reed, Rachel Reeves, Jonathan Rutherford, Mari Sako, Jørn Tomter, Mark Wickham-Jones, Patricia Williams, and Hughie Wong, from each of whom I learnt so much. Austin Hayden and Greg Hyman also provided brilliant editorial assistance.

I am also extraordinarily grateful to those I was lucky enough to learn from when I was working for Ed Miliband, including David Axelrod, Gurnek Bains, Tom Baldwin (again), Greg Beales, Torsten Bell, Jill Cuthbertson, Stan Greenberg, Rachel Kinnock, Tess Lanning, Spencer Livermore, Tim Livesey, James Morris, Harvey Redgrave, Anna Yearly, and, of course, Ed himself. As a speechwriter, I was fortunate to seek wisdom from James Graham, Paul Greengrass, and Josie Rourke. They taught me more than I could ever have imagined.

Finally, there are the four people who remain the closest. Lizzy Pellicano exemplifies so many of the virtues I try to praise in this book. Her work combining basic science with the everyday world of autistic advocacy is a daily inspiration to me. My mum, Jane Stears, keeps me grounded. She has chipped in with the really difficult questions all along the way, including the unbeatable, "Whatever happened to that book you were writing?" As my mum was all too aware, I started this book with my dad, Derek, and without my daughter, Freya. One has been an incalculable loss and the other an unimaginable gain. As every reader will be able to tell, my dad's spirit runs through every page of this text. He taught me to love creativity and to find it both in the treasured and in the most ordinary places. A day with him driving the backstreets of Cardiff, Newport, or Pontypool looking for a rugby ground was as uplifting as one in the Musée d'Orsay or the National Gallery. Freya's spirit is here too. She daily shows just how magical the ordinary can be, whether it be through a plastic seal putting on a show at bathtime or by making me be Mr. Tod to her Peter Rabbit and chasing her through the Botanic Gardens. No one exhibits as much power in the everyday as Freya. That's why this book is dedicated to her. At heart, it is my small effort to remember the best of the country from which I took her away. Perhaps, when she returns, the vision I describe will be there waiting for her again.

Index